COLD READING Games

Kickstart the conversation
and banish awkward silences forever!

More 'Speed Learning' by Julian Moore

More 'Speed Learning' by Julian Moore

Available from
The Cold Reading Company

www.thecoldreadingcompany.co.uk

DON'T FORGET TO DOWNLOAD YOUR <u>FREE</u>

CHEAT SHEET

SEE LAST PAGE OF THIS BOOK FOR DETAILS

~

This book contains extracts from previously published material in the 'Speed Learning' series by Julian Moore

Palmistry - Palm Readings In Your Own Words

Graphology - The Art Of Handwriting Analysis

Numerology - Numbers Past And Present With The Lo Shu Square

Star Signs - A Cool System For Remembering The Dates And Meanings Of The Twelve Signs Of The Zodiac

The James Bond Cold Reading

Cartomancy - Fortune Telling With Playing Cards

TABLE OF CONTENTS

Cold Reading Games

Who This Book Is For

This book is a social toolkit for guys who like girls, to give them the confidence to banish uncomfortable pauses and missed opportunities with members of the opposite sex forever

- Do you enjoy female company but sometimes find it difficult to strike up a conversation?

- Are you going on a date but you're a bit worried you'll run out of things to say?

- Or would you simply like to inject a little more fun into your social life?

If you answered yes to any of these questions then this book could be for you.

This book will teach you enough about Palmistry, Graphology and Numerology to get you into trouble. If you're looking for an in-depth guide to giving readings then you've most certainly come to the wrong place; unlike some of my other books this particular book is more about kickstarting conversations with an emphasis on 'talking the talk' in social situations.

This may not be a reference work yet the source material is taken from my previous 'Speed Learning' series of books that cover each topic in more detail, so even though these pages are high in theory and low in fact, all the descriptions in this book adhere to the commonly accepted meanings for each topic. What is presented here is a light-hearted approach to the real-deal, simplified so you can concentrate on having fun instead of getting bogged down in the intricacies of each system. Think of these techniques like 'get out of jail free' cards; if you become trapped in an awkward social situation you can try one out and, more often than not, become unstuck almost immediately.

Why Write This Book?

Over the years I've realised that many young (and not so young) men have bought my books, not because they'd like to be a palmist, graphologist, numerologist or even a reader of cards, but because they'd simply like to have a few skills that could help them out in social situations. This book addresses the need for an overview that brings these things together in a playful way for people that, initially at least, are more interested in creating conversations than becoming a reader of anything in particular. Knowing a little about these skills can be great fun, and in the right circumstances with the right people can help create a considerable amount of memorable moments, laughter, and even new friends.

Keep it light, do it right, and with a bit of luck you'll never be stuck for words again.

Learn to talk the talk and you'll be doing most of the listening.

Introduction

Whether you're on a first date or simply having a casual chat with a member of the opposite sex, most of us have lost our mojo at one time or another; the conversation stutters to a halt after a few uncomfortable silences and you're left wondering what to say or do next to keep things interesting. Even the most outgoing of people can run out of steam occasionally, and for the more introverted there can be little steam to start with.

Keeping things moving in these situations can be tricky. Of course, the best way to keep things interesting is to BE interesting, but that can be easier said than done.

Learning a few new skills to help you interact with people in a non-threatening way is a no-brainer. Palmistry and graphology are terrific ice-breakers that help lighten the mood and enable other people to talk about themselves, which as we all know is everybody's favourite subject. Nothing creates empathy more than being a good listener, and although your initial reaction may be to tell someone how great you are the moment you meet them, shifting the focus away from yourself is far more endearing and attractive. Confidence is less about telling people who you are, and more about knowing who you are and taking an interest in others.

Many of the resources on dating, chat up lines and PUA* often refer to cold reading, palmistry and graphology as good skills to have in reserve for those times where you'd like to create a shared moment with someone. Very few of these resources mention the best way to learn these skills, and when they do they often refer to books that go into way too much depth for the casual socialiser. This book has been created with one thing in mind; to give guys as much information as they need to get into trouble while teaching the real deal.

Pulled mainly from my other books on these subjects, this book's sole intention is to get you up to speed just enough for you to keep the conversation flowing. As this book is derived from my previous work and is based on tried and tested principles, what you learn here should you stand you in good stead further down the line. It also means that when you occasionally meet people who know more than you do about this stuff (and you will), you won't look stupid as what you're learning is 'true', in as much as it won't clash with other people's knowledge on these matters.

Unlike my other books that can get you on the road to being a pro or semi-pro in a relatively short period of time, this book is more about teaching you how to create interesting and fun moments where there would otherwise be awkward silences and lost opportunities to make new friends, and possibly more.

PUA actually stands for 'Pick Up Artist' and it a common abbreviation found in internet communities interested in these matters. Don't blame me, I just work here.

How To Use This Book

Although you may have bought this book with the idea of focusing on one specific topic, I encourage you to work through this book and learn things in order. Palmistry is the most tactile and therefore the most useful skill for our purposes, and the palmistry section has many concepts that will help you enormously as you work through the other chapters. It would be a waste of space to repeat similar concepts in one section that have already been covered in another, and many ideas that you'll learn about giving palmistry readings can be applied to graphology and beyond.

Getting Your Mouth In Gear

While you're learning from this book you're going to need to practice speaking out loud, as if you were giving someone a reading. It may feel strange at first, but you simply must get your mouth in gear and learn to shoot from the hip, thinking out loud and verbalising every idea and thought in your head as you think of them.

Throughout this book are questions that will put you on the spot and encourage you to verbalise what you are thinking. If you skip these exercises or decide to do them in your head you will simply not gain the confidence you need to be able to use these skills in the real world. Everything in this book is about communication, and as you're the one most likely to instigate a conversation with someone, you must be comfortable with the sound of your own voice and at least vaguely confident that you can keep going, even when things get tricky or awkward.

Speak out loud as often as you can while you work through this book and you'll be giving interesting, informal readings in no time.

A Quick Note About Cold Reading

What is 'cold reading'? Broadly speaking, cold reading attempts to address the science *behind* giving readings. It's a scientific look at 'what's actually going on' during a reading.

Shut-eyes (psychics who deny that psychology adds any weight to their readings) argue that they have 'the gift' and that people who dabble in cold reading are missing a vital psychic connection. Psychologists argue that cold reading is what's *really* happening during a reading with a 'psychic'; a simple succession of exchanges that give the reader the *appearance* of being psychic when in fact a series of clever, if unintended, psychological ploys are taking place.

All I know is that there are good readers and bad readers. Hopefully this book, regardless of its modus-operandi, will turn you into a good one.

Although there's no real reference to cold reading in this book, it's full of it. You'll learn to give readings that are fun and make sense, simply by using your own common sense. At no point will you be learning to tell people their future or pretending that you know 'all about them' when you don't. But as you read this book you'll realise that, although I'll be teaching you the historical meanings of these systems, the focus is always on connecting with people and having fun with both eyes wide open.

Three Skills

This book will teach you the basics of palmistry, graphology and numerology, but more importantly it will show you what to actually 'do' with this information. The focus here is on 'talking the talk' and less about gaining an encyclopaedic knowledge of any one thing. You're not claiming to be an authority on these subjects (in fact that's the last thing you want people to think), and in public you need to play your abilities down yet be willing to show people what you know in a fun and friendly way. Let's face it, it's all just a big excuse to practice your communication skills, and if you're still talking about palmistry or numerology at the end of a night out then something's probably gone horribly wrong. The point of this knowledge is to keep the conversation flowing, not hijack it by droning on about graphology until midnight. Although this knowledge can get you out of some tricky silences, you also need to learn when to shut up about it and let the conversation take its course.

Here's how palmistry, graphology, numerology and astrology can help you out when you're having one of those awkward moments:

Palmistry

Everyone has a palm, and even the most skeptical of people enjoy having their palm read. Nothing is required apart from someone's hand and a pair of eyes to see it. The only downside to reading someone's palm (and there are almost no downsides) is that the moment anyone sees you attempt a palm reading they'll probably want theirs read too. This can actually work to your advantage, as you'll discover later. Bear in mind that almost everyone knows that there is a head line and a heart line, and quite a few women will be more clued up about the lines of the hand than yourself.

Graphology

Not quite as direct as palmistry, graphology (or handwriting analysis) requires you to get someone to write their name down. It also gives you a good excuse to learn their name in the first place (and perhaps get their mobile number), useful if you're not on a date but attempting to set one up. You'll need at least a pen, and quite often a napkin or receipt to write on if you're in a public place like a bar or restaurant.

Numerology

The world pretty much revolves around mobile phones these days and by giving someone a little numerology reading based on their phone number you can, somewhat brazenly, give yourself a chance to text them later. Combine numerology with graphology and you have someone's name and their number.

As we can see from these descriptions, palmistry can be used to create a bit more intimacy on a date in progress, but is also spontaneous enough to be used casually with people you've only just met. Graphology is only slightly more involved as it requires actually writing things down so is generally better for dates, although it can be useful when combined with numerology to get someone's name and phone number.

One thing tends to lead to another, and a foray into the world of palmistry can often lead to graphology, numerology and all manner of other things. Just keep everything fun and light hearted and forget about impressing anyone. Even though you secretly might be.

Remember that these ruses are designed to create conversation, and a conversation is a two way street. You need to get the other person to talk by giving them the space to do so. It may feel unnatural to leave long gaps while you're talking, but you need to encourage other people to help you interpret what's in front of you, whether it's their palm, their handwriting or some numbers.

Every second the other person is doing the talking, you're winning. It's amazing how much empathy people feel towards those who take an interest.

Once again, the mantra of this book is: Learn to talk the talk and you'll be doing most of the listening.

Backstory

Where did you learn all this stuff?

Let's be honest, telling someone that you learnt palmistry from a book specifically about going on a date probably won't do you any favours. You're going to have to come up with a pretty good reason as to why you know any of this information. If you're over six foot tall and built like a heavyweight boxer you might find it difficult to convince someone that you're in touch with your 'feminine side'. You also most definitely don't want to say you learnt palmistry from an ex-girlfriend, as a date will probably be expecting something like that anyway. You're going to have to come up with some more believable reasons than 'I read about it in a book'.

Here are a few palmistry and graphology backstory ideas. Whatever you do, make your reasons interesting and vaguely plausible based on your current situation and who you are. Do yourself a favour and try and make yourself look good at the same time too.

It's really important that you give this some proper thought; it will help your readings, give you confidence and will be one less thing to worry about.

Palmistry Backstories

"I went on holiday with some friends a few years back, and there was a palmistry book knocking about in the house we rented together. It kept getting pulled out in the late evenings when we'd had one too many drinks. It's probably all nonsense, but it's good fun."

"There was an old guy on the beach in Goa giving palm readings for a few coins. I looked some of it up when I got back home to see if he'd just made it up. It's quite interesting really."

"My grandma used to read tea leaves and she had an old bookcase with lots of strange and interesting books in it. I used to flick through some of them as a kid, the palmistry one was always fun as it had the most pictures."

Of course I've made these up as examples, but there's a vague bit of truth in all of them for me personally. I've gone on holidays with friends in rented houses, I've been to Goa and I do have a grandmother who used to read tea leaves. Elaborate on your own truths and you'll be comfortable with your personal (albeit 'made up') reasons for knowing this stuff.

Graphology Backstories

There's a bit more scope with the reasoning for knowing about graphology as it's seen as more of a science, and possibly a bit more of a 'guy thing'. Very few people know much about graphology, yet most people would find handwriting analysis 'believable', even useful. It's the kind of stuff you hear people talk about in recruitment, see in films and read about in crime novels. So how come you know so much about it?

"I was sat next to a guy on a plane once who was a forensics expert. He got me to write my signature down on a napkin and told me a few things about myself which were pretty accurate! I've been kind of interested in it ever since."

"I had a friend who used to collect autographs after he inherited some from his grandmother. We used to look through them and he got into the whole handwriting thing, I was into it too for a bit."

"There was a whodunnit on TV where they analysed someone's handwriting to catch the killer. I wonder if I can tell if you're a natural born killer?"

Of course this last one is slightly ridiculous, but quite good fun. Don't forget to have fun.

Your Stories

So there's a few ideas to get you going, but what's YOUR story? Make sure to make one up for each skill; you'll feel happier if you do and it will make the whole experience a lot more believable for you and the people you meet. You'll also feel a lot more confident with a believable backstory and like I said before, try to create a story that makes you sound interesting and look good! You'll find cynics who will call you out on your new found abilities, so it's better to be prepared.

Things To Do

Before you go any further, create your own backstory for each skill. Try to come up with unforgettable ideas, including things that reflect your own life and interests, and don't be afraid to stretch the truth a little to make yourself look good. If possible, write them down.

- I know a few things about Palmistry because...
- I know a bit about Graphology because...
- I picked up some knowledge about Numerology when...
- I learned about Astrology when...

Palmistry

Some of the material in this chapter is taken from my book 'Palmistry - Palm Readings In Your Own Words'

You'll find that quite a few women have a passing knowledge of palmistry, even if the most they've done is checked the lines of their own hand with a moth-eaten palmistry book. In a casual setting it's unlikely that anyone is going to expect you to tell them their future; most people are simply expecting to be told about their personality. So it's more a question of what am I like and less about what's going to happen.

Let's not forget your knowledge of palmistry is something you've picked up along your travels and you're not professing to be an authority on the subject. In fact, I'd keep away from the idea of 'fortune telling' altogether and focus solely on the idea that a person's hand can reveal something about their personality. Occasionally people will take you rather seriously and ask to know something about their future, and in these situations it's best to explain that you don't read people's fortunes.

Before we learn about the lines of the hand, let's put ourselves in the right frame of mind and spend a moment thinking about how we're going to act when we're giving a reading.

Talk The Talk - But Remember To Listen

When you first start looking at someone's palm they're likely to say very little and expect you to do all the talking. To get the conversation moving you need to ask leading questions every once in a while, such as 'Does that make sense to you?' and 'Do you agree?', to let the person know that they're expected to join in. Initially they'll probably reply with very short 'yes' and 'no' answers, but as you continue to talk more about their hand they'll become more involved, and quite often ask for clarifications. Funnily enough, it's usually when you're telling them things that they don't agree with that they'll chime in. Being 'wrong' doesn't matter (it's what the hand is telling you), and conversation is conversation whether someone agrees with you or not; what's important is to create dialogue. Just make sure to leave lots of pauses to goad some kind of response from the person whose hand you are looking at as often as you can.

Don't forget to talk to the person too, and not just their hand. Take time to look up and engage in conversation, their hand will still be there when you look down again. Focus on their hand, but not too much. Remember to focus on 'them' while you're at it. A little eye contact never went amiss, and by actually looking at the person face to face you'll be able to assess their reaction to you and your reading. If you spend the whole time focussed on their hand exclusively you'll miss all kinds of smiles, frowns and quizzical looks that can help you gauge your progress as you concoct your dialogue.

Let's not forget that the whole point of giving a palm reading in the context of this book is to be sociable and have some fun. If you don't manage to talk about everything you've learned in these pages because the conversation has veered off onto more interesting topics then you've succeeded in being engaging, entertaining and interesting. That's all that matters.

What you're really trying to do is to get people to talk about themselves, and you can't listen if you're talking the whole time

The Only Girl In The World

Remember that everyone wants to feel like they have the most interesting palm in the world, so if you see anything unusual in anyones hand, point it out! Not only that, no matter what is going on around you, make the person whose hand you a looking at the sole focus of your attention.

Be positive, upbeat and lighthearted about all of this. Make people feel good, interesting, and unique. For our purposes, palm reading is an exercise in having some fun, so don't come across as too serious or intense. You're not claiming to be a professional, just a cool guy that is relaxed around women and doesn't mind spreading a bit of knowledge that he's picked up on his travels. Keep it light.

Remember to give people your undivided attention and do anything you can to make them feel special

See You Later, Alligator

If someone else sees you giving a palm reading, there's a good chance they'll want their own palm read too. Rejection is tantamount to being told you're not interesting, so be careful not to upset anyone by turning down their request for a palm reading. You can always say you'll read their palm later, a promise they will very rarely forget.

In fact, if you're really interested in someone who wants a palm reading but you're too busy (possibly with someone else's palm!), a good way to make sure you see them again is to promise them a reading later on. They will not forget this and will track you down shortly, possibly with some friends in tow, which is always a nice position to find yourself in!

Smile, have fun and be courteous to everyone, even if they're not the object of your affections; everyone loves a gentleman

Now let's move on to the basics of palmistry that most people know something about; the heart, head and life lines.

The Heart Line, Head Line and Life Line

Knowing the meanings of the three main lines is essential as they are the starting point for talking about someone's palm:

The Heart Line is the top line nearest the fingers, and represents the EMOTIONS

The Head Line is the middle line and represents the THOUGHT PROCESS

The Life Line is the bottom line that curves around the thumb, and represents VITALITY or life energy

Find each line on your own hand, and notice how long each one is, the curve they take and which fingers they end up under.

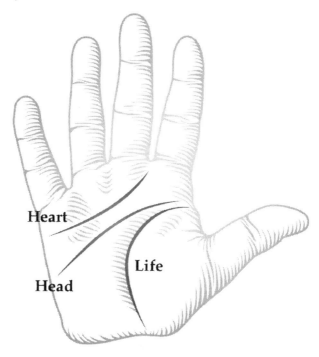

For instance, my heart line ends under my forefinger, and curves slightly upwards towards the fingers. My heart line slants down and stop about three quarters of the way down my hand below the joint of my third and fourth fingers, and my life line sweeps down and around to the centre of my hand where it splits, the main line curving right around the base of my thumb and another fainter line continuing onwards towards my wrist for about a centimetre.

By comparing the size, length and start and end points of the lines on the hand we have something to talk about. Many people know this stuff already, so it's important you learn this 'common knowledge' so you don't end up looking silly in front of someone who knows more than you. What you're learning here is the standard meanings of the lines, so you can be rest assured that they will match up with the expectations of those who already know a thing or two about palmistry.

TOP TIP: The longer a line, the more of that trait someone possesses. For instance, a long heart line shows high emotions, a shorter one shows a colder person. A long life line shows lots of energy, a short one someone who is lacking energy. Slightly different is the head line; a long line shows a detailed thinker, a shorter one a quick thinker.

Comparisons - The Crux Of Any Reading

What most laypeople DON'T realise is that the real fun starts when you compare the lines of the hand with one another. The meanings of the lines often contradict each other and comparing their differences can give us a great deal to talk about. Don't forget, we are learning to say a lot from very little in this book as our main aim is to create conversation with as little knowledge as possible. We don't want to distract ourselves with too many facts! We want to learn a few facts and get as much conversational mileage out of them as possible. If you know too much you'll be thinking too hard and talking less, so for our purposes it's better to know less and talk more.

Now let's take a look at each line on the hand individually.

Heart Line
Emotions

The heart line is the 'top' line of the hand nearest the fingers. It deals with the emotions. We are looking at the way the line curves and where it ends to glean two pieces of information.

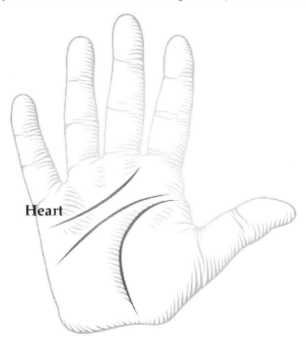

Does the heart line run in a straight line across the hand, or does it bend upwards towards the fingers?

- Heart line bends towards fingers = Open hearted / Expressive

17

• Heart line runs straight across palm = Less expressive / More sensitive and needy

TOP TIP: We use our fingers to reach out and touch the world around us so a heart line that turns up towards the fingers shows a need to communicate and a heart line that goes straight across the hand is less communicative.

Where does the heart line end?

A long heart line shows an emotionally open individual, a short heart line shows an emotionally closed loner.

• Heart line ends beneath 1st finger (LONG LINE) = Emotionally open / Romantically idealistic

• Heart line ends beneath 2nd finger (SHORT LINE) = Emotionally closed / Loner

• Somewhere in-between 1st and 2nd finger (AVERAGE LINE) = Emotionally balanced

Curve vs Length

There may be contradictions in this one line alone. For instance, a heart line that bends towards the fingers (open hearted and expressive) but is rather short (emotionally closed) could show someone who is all open arms when they first meet someone, but as soon as they get too close they simply shut down emotionally. If you can think of something to say when you've only got one line to work with, you'll have plenty to talk about when you compare the characteristics of all three lines!

The art of giving a reading is to think out loud while trying to make sense of the similarities and contradictions you see whilst encouraging a response.

IN A NUTSHELL

A long heart line that bends up towards the fingers shows someone who is emotionally open and romantic

which is the opposite of

A short heart line that runs straight across the hand; someone emotionally closed and perhaps a loner

Heart Line Questions - See if you can answer these questions before you move on

The first six questions are simply about getting your facts right. The last four questions are about talking the talk, so attempt to answer them OUT LOUD as if you were actually talking to someone.

1. There are three main lines on the hand. Where is the heart line positioned?

2. If someone has a long heart line, what does it mean?

3. What does it mean if someone has a heart line that ends beneath their second finger?

4. Someone's heart line goes straight across their palm, what does it mean?

5. What does it mean if someone has a short heart line?

6. What does it mean if someone's heart line curves up towards their fingers?

7. You notice that someone's heart line is quite short, yet curves towards their fingers. What could you say to them? (Say this out loud)

8. Someone's heart line is quite long and straight. What could you say about it? (Say this out loud)

9. You are holding a hand whose heart line is short and straight. Describe what that means. (Say this out loud)

10. A girl shows you a palm that has a long heart line that curves almost right up to their fingers. What could you say to her about it? (Say this out loud)

You may know what the various types of heart line mean, but it's learning to talk about it that's important. You may have struggled with verbalising the last four questions, but with practice and a couple of other lines to talk about you'll have plenty of ammunition.

Read through this section about the heart line again, and when you go through the questions a second time try to see how long you can talk out loud when you're answering the last four verbalised questions.

If you're happy with what you've learned about the heart line, let's move on to the next line, the head line.

Head Line
Thought Process

The head line runs across the middle line of the hand and represents the thought process. We are looking at the way the line curves down across the palm, how long it is and also how close it is to the other lines on the hand.

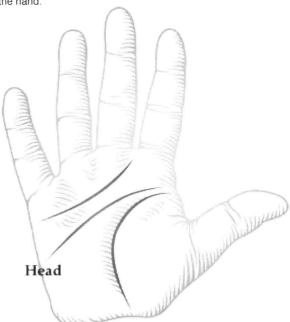

Does the head line run in a straight line across the hand or does it curve down towards the wrist?

In a similar way to the heart line, the curve in the head line is important. If the head line runs straight across the palm keeping towards the finger side of the hand, the thought processes are drawn towards practicalities. If the head line curves away from the fingers somewhat towards the wrist, the thought process are reflected inwards to the more creative inner self.

• Head line curves to wrist = Creative

• Head line is straight across palm = Logical / Down to earth

TOP TIP: If a head line curves inward towards the body the person is more inwardly creative, whereas a head line that is more towards the fingers is more practical and down to earth.
How long is the head line?

This is pretty straightforward; the longer the head line, the longer the person takes to think things through, a short line showing a quicker thinker than someone with a longer line.

• Short = Quick thinker

• Long = Detailed thinker

How close is the head line to the heart line?

Here we bring the idea of the first two lines together. If the heart and head line touch then it stands to reason that the person's heart and head are tangled, somewhat impulsive. If they're separate then the person manages to keep his heart and head apart.

• Head line touches heart line = Impulsive

• Head line separate from heart line = Cautious

IN A NUTSHELL

A head line runs across the hand in more practical people, and bends towards the wrist in more creative people

The length of the head line shows the speed of someone's thought process

Head Line Questions - See if you can answer these questions before you move on

1. Where is the head line positioned on the hand?

2. If someone has a long head line, what does it mean?

3. If someone's head line curves towards their wrist, what does it mean?

4. What does it mean if someone has a short head line?

5. Someone's head line is tangled with their heart line. What does that mean?

6. What would it mean if their head and heart lines were completely separate?

7. What would you say to someone who had a short head line? (Say this out loud)

8. What could you say to someone who had a head line that went straight across their hand? (Say this out loud)

9. You meet a girl who has a very long head line that curves down towards her wrist. What would you say to her? (Say this out loud)

10. You meet someone who has a short head line, yet it curves down towards her wrist. You also notice that it is tangled with her heart line. What could you say about it all? (Say this out loud)

You've probably noticed that I'm making the questions slightly more complex, simply by asking you to combine the ideas from each line together. As you can see, this can either give you complimentary ideas, or contradictory ideas. See how you get on with these questions for now, we'll get on to more expansive answers in a slightly later chapter.

Read through this section about the head line again, making a special point of trying to say as much as you can when you verbalise the questions.

If you're happy with what you've learned about the head line, let's move on to the last line, the life line.

Life Line
Vitality

Generally speaking, the more of an arc the life line takes around the base of the thumb, the longer the line is. We are looking at the length of the line, and where it starts.

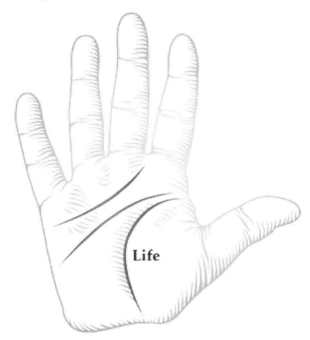

How wide does the life line sweep around the base of the thumb?

People with long life lines that take a large arc around the thumb have a lot of vitality and energy, whereas people with small life lines that hug the thumb can be quite lethargic.

· Life line takes a large arc (LONG) = Energy

· Life line hugs the thumb (SHORT) = Lacking energy

Where does the life line start?

As we've discovered with the heart line, being nearer the fingers means 'more outgoing' and the life line is no exception.

· A life line that starts near the first finger = Ambitious

· A life line that starts close to the thumb = Humble

· A life line that starts somewhere between the first finger and thumb = Practical

IN A NUTSHELL

The length of someone's life line shows how much energy they have

The nearer their lifeline starts to the fingers, the more ambitious they are

Life Line Questions - See if you can answer these questions before you move on

1. Where is the life line positioned on the hand?

2. If someone has a short life line, what does it mean?

3. What does it mean if someone has a life line that starts quite far from their fingers?

4. What does a long life line signify?

5. If someone's life line starts near the fingers, what does it mean?

6. You meet someone who has a long life line that starts somewhere between their first finger and thumb. What could you say to them? (Say this out loud)

7. A girl shows you her hand and it has a short life line that starts near her fingers. What would you say to her? (Say this out loud)

8. You are presented with a hand that shows a medium length life line that starts a fair distance away from the fingers. What could you say to this person? (Say this out loud)

9. You are looking at a long life line that starts close to the fingers. What could you say to its owner? (Say this out loud)

10. You meet someone whose life line starts between their first finger and thumb and is of average length. What could you say about it? (Say this out loud)

As you have probably noticed, there is less information on the life line than the other two lines. Also, it's possible that you may have found it tricky to verbalise question 8 and even harder to verbalise question 10 as both of these hands are fairly nondescript with 'average' lines, neither long nor small. Something you're going to have to get used to is that in the real world, the lines on people's hands tend to be far less clear cut or obvious; very often you'll struggle to judge whether a line is long or short, curved or straight. This is why it's so important to practice getting your mouth in gear by talking out loud, and of course the best way to do this is to practice on real people. Luckily the whole point of this book is to come up with excuses to socialise, and what better excuse than to admit that you're a novice and need the practice!

Read through this section about the life line again, making a special point of trying to say as much as you can when you verbalise the questions.

Lines Recap

Let's condense the information for the three lines into an easy to remember list:

Heart Line - EMOTIONS (top line, nearest to fingers)

A long heart line that bends up towards the fingers shows someone who is emotionally open and romantic

which is the opposite of

A short heart line that runs straight across the hand; someone emotionally closed and perhaps a loner

Head Line - THOUGHT PROCESS (middle line)

A head line has no curve in practical people, but curves towards the wrist in more creative people

The length of the head line shows how long a person takes to think

A head line that touches the heart line shows an impulsive person

Life Line - VITALITY (curves around the base of the thumb)

The length of someone's life line shows how much energy they have

The nearer their lifeline starts to the fingers, the more ambitious they are

Things to remember:

With all lines, towards the fingers = more outgoing / away from the fingers = less outgoing

Similarly, towards the fingers = practical / away from the fingers = more creative and inward

Longer lines = more of a trait / shorter lines = less of a trait

For example:

- Long heart line = lot of heart (open and romantic) / short heart line = less heart (more introverted)

- Long head line = methodical thinker / short head line = quick thinker

- Long life line = lots of energy / short life line = less energy

TOP TIP: If you're ever struggling to read the lines on someone's hand don't be afraid to straighten their hand or cup their palm to give you more information. Even the faintest of lines can become more apparent when the hand is cupped slightly.

In a moment, we'll cover how to talk about this information in an interesting way. You'll be amazed how much mileage you can get from just three simple lines, and your ability to talk freely about all three together will set you apart from most people's palm reading attempts. Let's stick with each line individually before we move on, and see if we can remember everything we've learned so far by doing all of the previous questions in one go.

Test Recap

Here are the previous 30 palmistry questions, scrambled up with the ones that need verbalising at the end. See if you can get through all of them in one go.

While trying to answer the questions out loud there will be moments when you run out of words but KEEP TALKING AS LONG AS YOU CAN. If you can't talk to an empty room you'll struggle with a real person.

If you do get a little stuck, just remember these two simple rules:

· The longer a line, the more of that trait someone has

· Lines that curve towards the fingers are more practical, lines that curve towards the wrist are more creative and introverted

Remembering these two simple rules is usually enough to jog your memory should you get stuck.

QUESTIONS

1. There are three main lines on the hand. Where is the head line positioned?

2. Where is the heart line positioned?

3. Where is the life line positioned?

4. If someone has a long heart line, what does it mean?

5. What does it mean if someone has a short head line?

6. What does a long life line signify?

7. What does it mean if someone has a short heart line?

8. If someone has a long head line, what does it mean?

9. If someone has a short life line, what does it mean?

10. Someone's head line is tangled with their heart line. What does that mean?

11. What does it mean if someone has a life line that starts quite far from their fingers?

12. Someone's heart line goes straight across their palm, what does it mean?

13. If someone's head line curves towards their wrist, what does it mean?

24

14. What would it mean if their head and heart lines were completely separate?

15. If someone's life line starts near the fingers, what does it mean?

16. What does it mean if someone's heart line curves up towards their fingers?

17. What does it mean if someone has a heart line that ends beneath their second finger?

18. You meet someone who has a long life line that starts somewhere between their first finger and thumb. What could you say to them? (Say this out loud)

19. A girl shows you her hand and it has a short life line that starts near her fingers. What would you say to her? (Say this out loud)

20. You are presented with a hand that shows a medium length life line that starts a fair distance away from the fingers. What could you say to this person? (Say this out loud)

21. You are looking at a long life line that starts close to the fingers. What could you say to its owner? (Say this out loud)

22. You meet someone whose life line starts between their first finger and thumb and is of average length. What could you say about it? (Say this out loud)

23. You notice that someone's heart line is quite short, yet curves towards their fingers. What could you say to them? (Say this out loud)

24. Someone's heart line is quite long and straight. What could you say about it? (Say this out loud)

25. You are holding a hand whose heart line is short and straight. Describe what that means. (Say this out loud)

26. A girl shows you a palm that has a long heart line that curves almost right up to their fingers. What could you say to her about it? (Say this out loud)

27. What would you say to someone who had a short head line? (Say this out loud)

28. What could you say to someone who had a head line that went straight across their hand? (Say this out loud)

29. You meet a girl who has a very long head line that curves down towards her wrist. What would you say to her? (Say this out loud)

30. You meet someone who has a short head line, yet it curves down towards her wrist. You also notice that it is tangled with her heart line. What could you say about it all? (Say this out loud)

You don't have to be 100% perfect, but if you're fairly confident in answering most of these questions it's time to look at how to combine the information on all three lines to create an interesting moment with someone.

Bringing The Lines Together

Now you've got a basic understanding of the meanings of the three lines it's time to talk about all of them together. In the previous chapters I mentioned that looking for contradictions is an extremely important part of finding things to talk about. When you've got three lines to discuss it gets a lot easier; more lines, more contradictions.

Let's look at an example of a hand whose traits have similar tendencies; a long heart line that curves towards the fingers, that doesn't touch a long head line that curves towards the wrist and a long life line that starts somewhere between the thumb and first finger.

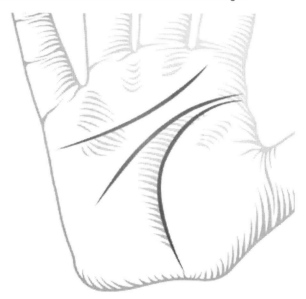

- Long heart line that curves towards the fingers = emotionally open and romantic
- Heart and head line not touching = nothing
- Long head line that curves towards the wrist = creative, detailed thinker
- Long life line that starts somewhere between the first finger and thumb = energetic and practical

This leaves us with:

- Emotionally open and romantic
- Creative, detailed thinker
- Energetic and practical

If we look these traits we have someone who is emotionally open and romantic, creative, a detailed thinker who is practical. These traits are all fairly complimentary. You may think that's preferable than a hand full of contradictions, but once you start interpreting a hand whose traits are mostly complimentary you can quickly find yourself running out of things to talk about. Contradictions are far more useful as they bring up questions and demand answers you can discuss with the person whose hand you're looking at.

Gold Mining

Time for an analogy. If you've read any of my other books, you'll know I like an analogy:

A smooth surface in a goldmine doesn't give much up. What you're looking for is fissures; cracks in the rock face that reveal seams rich in gold. It's the same when giving a reading; the cracks deliver the most gold, and to find a seam rich for mining you need to look for the places where there is natural pressure. For us as readers, contradictions are our gold veins, opening up possibilities wherever they are found. If you look for irregularities, you'll find gold.

The idea is to look for conflicting elements in the lines and interpret them as you find them, thinking out loud and encouraging the person whose palm you are reading to join in, either by agreeing or disagreeing with you. Your interpretations are up for discussion so you will need to pause a moment for the person to digest what you have said after each one. Don't be afraid to say whatever springs to mind however; giving a reading is a two person process and to read someone's palm you need their help, so give them the space to think and react.

Here's something I said back in the 'Heart Line' section:

The art of giving a reading is to think out loud while trying to make sense of the similarities and contradictions you see whilst encouraging a response

As you work through this book and get some real-world experience, you'll appreciate this simple formula.

The basic concept is this:

1. Tell people what you can see (the 'facts')
2. Offer your interpretation of the facts
3. Wait for a reaction

Here's a recap of the 'complimentary' hand I mentioned earlier, and then an example reading. I've emboldened the parts where I am actively looking for comparisons and contradictions to give you an idea of where the gold is. Of course this text doesn't allow for the fact that giving a reading is a two way street and you'll be talking about the hand with the person and not just at the person. For now it'll give you a basic idea of what's going on and what to look out for.

• Long heart line that curves towards the fingers = emotionally open and romantic
• Heart and head line not touching = nothing
• Long head line that curves towards the wrist = creative, detailed thinker
• Long life line that starts somewhere between the first finger and thumb = energetic and practical

So basically, we're left with:

• Emotionally open and romantic
• Creative, detailed thinker
• Energetic and practical

'This is your heart line. People with short heart lines tend to be quite closed but you have a long heart line that reaches right over here to your first finger, showing that you're quite open hearted. This heart line also curves towards your fingers, which can make you a little romantically idealistic. So this could mean that you appear to be an open book to some people as you're quite outgoing, yet you have a tendency to be rather picky when it comes to boyfriends. [PAUSE]

'You have a nice long head line that sweeps down here towards your wrist, and this is definitely the line of a creative person, as people whose head lines tend to be somewhat inward in their own creative thoughts. [PAUSE]

'That's interesting isn't it, you've got this inwards creative streak yet as we saw in your heart line you're outgoing and open. Perhaps sometimes you find it hard to strike a balance between your outgoing side and your quieter creative side? [PAUSE]

'You've got this long life line so you're not lacking in energy for whatever you want to do, and as it starts here kind of between the thumb and first finger you're quite practical when you want to be, and not always lost in a creative haze. [PAUSE]

'Does any of that make sense to you?'

Of course in the real world these pauses won't be stony silences but conversations, quite short initially but getting longer as the whole hand is discussed and the person opens up.

Negative Then Positive

Whenever you can, explain the meaning of each line before interpreting it. You'll notice early on in the reading that I say 'People with short heart lines tend to be quite closed but you have a long heart line...' This is not only a good way to flesh out the reading and make you look like you know what you're talking about, but it also helps you reinforce your own knowledge of the lines of the hand as you go. Spreading a little knowledge is a good thing, and if you explain what you can see from the outset you'll prevent yourself from standing in silence while you hold someone's hand deep in thought.

TOP TIP: Holding a relative stranger's hand in silence while you stare at it is creepy. Be chatty, not creepy.

Taking this idea further, discussing a line's negative aspect ('short heart lines tend to be quite closed') but ending with its positive aspect ('but you have a long heart line that reaches right over here to your first finger, showing that you're quite open hearted') can be extremely flattering. Anything you can do to make a reading positive is a good thing, and as people don't know what you can see on their hand it's always worth pointing out the negative aspect of a line first, before telling someone they possess the positive aspect of that line. This is especially useful for hands whose lines are largely complimentary where you'd struggle to find things to say.

Taking this idea further still, you can counterbalance any negative trait on the hand with any positive trait. This is where the real gold is.

For example:

'You could be a bit like this, but you make up for it with this'

or

'You tend to be a bit like this, but luckily you have an abundance of this'

The reality is that you're not always going to get super confident, outgoing people. There are people out there who are defined by their insecurities and won't be afraid to admit it. In these cases you shouldn't be afraid to agree with them, but you should look for the positive traits that 'make up' for their deficiencies.

For example:

'So this means you tend to be a bit quiet and introverted, but you more than make up for it with a huge amount of inner determination, shown by this'

As you can see I'm not giving concrete examples here, I'm trying to get you thinking in the right way so you can deal with anything that's thrown at you, no matter what you see on someone's hand. The 'facts' are simply a catalyst; it's how you interact with someone to 'figure out' what it all means that's important. It's about learning the process more than the knowledge.

Linking Lines

Zooming in on each aspect of the hand individually helps you remember what to say and gives the reading a nice structure, but you need to link these ideas together by zooming out and looking at the bigger picture wherever you can.

For instance, no sooner am I talking about the second line in the example I say "You have a nice long head line that sweeps down here towards your wrist, and this is definitely the line of a creative person... That's interesting isn't it, you've got this inwards creative streak yet as we saw in your heart line you're outgoing and open."

As you can see I'm comparing the second line to the first line as a comparison with my interpretation "Perhaps sometimes you find it hard to strike a balance between your outgoing side and your quieter creative side?" By creating these types of links between the lines you can build up an interesting and fairly complex pattern of connections that will help describe the person.

The more hands you see the easier this will become. Treat each new hand as a treasure hunt and don't be afraid to ask questions and try to tie everything together as you go. Zoom in for the small stuff, but zoom out regularly whenever you feel you can connect traits from different lines and give a more general overview.

Person Versus Hand

You shouldn't be worried if the person disagrees with anything you say as there is no real thing as 'failure' when you're trying to interpret someone's palm. In fact, someone's opinion versus the 'factual' meaning of a line can be treated like another gold seam; you have their verbalised opinion versus the meaning of a line, and you can look to the other lines to try and find a 'reason' for it. As we've discussed, contradictions are where the gold is, and a person's opinion of herself versus a line on her hand is simply another contradiction. Perhaps she was more like her hand when she was younger, but changed? Perhaps she's scared to admit just how like her hand she is? Or perhaps you've both interpreted it slightly the wrong way?

Talk about the hand, talk about the contradictions and try to work it out with the person; you're both exploring her hand and you're merely a guide. If the person tells you that something you've said is incorrect and this leads to further conversation and analysis, you're getting somewhere; a reading is all about communication.

TOP TIP: Beware the silent ones. Giving a reading to someone who says absolutely nothing at all, letting you talk at length before finally turning around to all her friends to tell them how inaccurate you are is something you really need to watch out for. The people who pipe up and disagree with you are easy, as they're able to have a conversation; it's the quiet ones you've got to be wary of! At all costs, try and get people to talk, and if people won't talk don't give them too much information. Simply keep the reading short.

Taking this idea further, you should always trust your own intuition, regardless of what someone's palm tells you. Here's a quote from one of my favourite comedians:

'You can tell a lot about someone, by what they're like' - Harry Hill

What I'm getting at here is to rely on your common sense. If you're holding the hand of a confident, assured and obviously successful woman, yet her hand traits are showing you a lack of ambition or energy, you should remember that you're not reading a disembodied palm in a vacuum and that each hand is very much connected to a person! Instead of blindly going into the whole 'this line says this' routine, do yourself a favour and take the person's general look and attitude into account before you even open your mouth:

'I can see that you're a confident and assured lady and you've had your fair share of success, but it hasn't always been that way judging from this line here. Sometimes you've had to do everything you can to become the person you are today.'

If you simply apply the obvious you'll come out sounding a whole lot smarter, the reading will make more sense and the whole thing will feel a lot more organic. There's no hurry. Give yourself the time to think.

Finger Meanings

Most people know something about the lines of the hand but not that many people know much about the meanings of the fingers. Just like each line, the fingers have specific traits and they are extremely easy to remember, yet great fun to talk about.

Each finger represents a particular attribute, and their length and bend alter their interpretation accordingly. Luckily for us, the finger meanings give us an easy to use acronym, ARCC - Ambition, Responsibility, Creativity and Communication. As the fingers of the hand naturally create an arc when you hold them out, it couldn't be easier to remember!

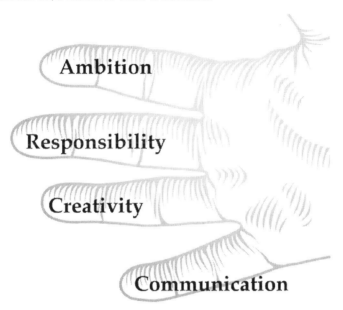

1st Finger - AMBITION
This is your pointing finger, it shows direction, YOUR direction and the things you want to achieve.

2nd Finger - RESPONSIBILITY
With the second finger you can make a very rude gesture (giving someone the finger!), but you have the choice to be rude or keep calm. This reminds us of the idea of personal responsibility.

3rd Finger - CREATIVITY
Only the most creative of people such as musicians and artists tend to use their third finger, for most it's a source of untapped potential.

4th Finger - COMMUNICATION
You can remember the fourth finger is communication by holding an 'imaginary telephone' to your head, listening to your thumb while you speak into your little finger.

So there we have the **ARCC** idea:

Ambition

Responsibility

Creativity

Communication

Interpreting The Fingers

When judging the length and size of someone's fingers it is entirely relative to their own hand. Is one of the fingers noticeably longer than average for that type of finger? Or is one of the fingers shorter for that type of finger? If the length isn't giving you any clues, look at the thickness of the fingers. Is one finger thicker or thinner than another?

As you can guess by now, the longer or bigger a finger is, the more its traits have dominance. Someone with a longer or bigger than average second finger is a responsible type and gets though life by using common sense. Conversely, someone with a noticeably small second finger can tend to be irresponsible and rash.

When you're judging the length and size of each finger it's often useful to straighten the palm out and push the fingers lightly together. When you're judging the bend in each finger it's useful to look for gaps between the fingers not only when the palm is straightened, but also when it is relaxed and at rest.

Another very important thing to look out for is for the curve and bend in peoples fingers. A bend in the finger weakens it slightly, and if one finger is leaning towards another it is leaning on that finger's trait to compensate for its own weakness. This is not necessarily a bad thing and simply shows which traits the person has leant on throughout their life. There is a lot of gold here! Weaknesses in one finger are compensated for by another, and this can all feed in to the information we have about the lines of the hand, which adds even more to our discussion.

Time for one of my analogies. I like analogies.

The Palm Tree Analogy

Imagine that the fingers are four palm trees in a line. The strongest tree stands completely straight, and the other trees bend towards it for protection. Some fingers are dominant, and the other fingers lean in that direction to make up for their own weaknesses.

For example, a someone may have a strong third finger (creativity) but their second finger (responsibility) bends towards it. This could show someone whose creativity makes up for their lack of responsibility.

As another example, someone could have a strong second finger (responsibility) but their first finger (ambition) bends towards it. This could show someone whose responsible outlook overshadows their ambition.

By combining this finger information with the lines of the hand we have more traits to compare and discuss.

The Approach

This section is solely for people you've met casually, such as in a bar or club. If you're already on a date, you're not going to need to do this. Hopefully!

One minute you're standing there feeling a bit awkward, the next minute you're talking to a female while you hold their hand and talk about palmistry. How?

First and foremost, you need to 'notice' someone's hand. This sounds pretty ridiculous as everyone has hands. Fortunately women generally take good care of their hands and will, more often than not, be wearing rings and possibly have painted nails or even false nails. Women see their hands as part of their natural beauty, so complimenting someone's hands for any reason is a very nice thing to say and is also an incredibly safe compliment, if a little unusual. Unusual is good, and a compliment is a compliment.

Of course every situation is different and you're going to have to use a little common sense. But generally the idea is to pay someone a slightly off-the-wall compliment, and add some kind of meaning to it.

An Example

You're having a slightly awkward moment at a bar with a girl you hardly know, and she's a bit quiet and not really engaging with you. Your friends have disappeared into the throng and left you alone with this girl, and she's obviously feeling a little awkward too. You'd like to get to know her better.

You take an obvious interest in her hands by occasionally staring down at them, to the point where it's been acknowledged and is perhaps a little strange.

Girl: (looking down a few times to see what you're looking at) 'Are you staring at my handbag?'

You: (smiling) 'No, at your hands! I'm looking at your fingers, they're really slender.'

Girl: (somewhat taken aback) 'Oh, thanks!' (awkward pause) 'So what?'

You: 'People with slender fingers tend to be quite creative. I just wondered if you were an artist or something, or did something creative?'

Girl: 'Oh, what else can you tell?' (offers you her hand)

This may look utterly ridiculous on the page, but the idea isn't. You probably wouldn't have to ask for her hand; it would be offered. No matter how strange this may seem to start with, if you end with a compliment then you can't go wrong.

Another Example

A girl you quite like who's with a group of people you've somehow managed to side up to in a club is checking her mobile phone. She's got pretty impressive false nails which are fairly obvious as he's holding her phone up to her face to read the screen.

You: 'Your nails are cool, how long does it take to get those nails on every day?'

Girl: (lowering phone) 'Huh? Oh, I dunno, twenty minutes?'

You: 'You've got really long fingers, those nails make them look even longer! People with long fingers are really creative. Are you an artist or something?'

33

Girl: (laughs) 'No! I work in a shop. Why? Are you some kind of guru?'

You: (smiling) 'No, but can I take a look at your hand? I think it might be interesting.'

Girl: (putting phone away) 'Sure, go ahead!' (offers you her hand)

Sometimes you have to be a bit more upfront as in this example. The main idea is that it doesn't really matter how strange your behaviour or interest, the moment people realise they might have someone read their palm they won't care how upfront you've been. Being told all about yourself is exciting.

Every situation and person is different, and it would be impossible (and utterly ludicrous) for me to attempt to describe every potential scenario that could crop up in the pages of this book; simply use these ideas as a springboard, and find out what works for you by actually trying. I think you'll be amazed with what you come up with on the spur of the moment! Don't worry about it too much; no matter what you say remember to end with a compliment and you'll be fine.

Be Creative

Everyone likes to think they're creative. If you tell someone you think they're creative and they actually turn out to be an artist, musician or some other creative type of person then you're already looking pretty good. The other good thing about creativity is that EVERYONE thinks they're creative, and even the most non-creative people on earth believe they have some deep untapped creative potential hiding in them somewhere. So the word 'creative' is very useful as it always comes across as a compliment and people tend to connect their own beliefs about themselves to it.

WHATEVER you say about someone's hand to get their attention, say something about creativity. You can even make it up.

• 'I like the way you've painted your nails. It's really creative.'

• 'You have really soft looking hands. Are you an artist or something?'

• 'I like your ring, did you make it yourself? Your hand looks very creative.'

Again, you need to pick up on anything strange or interesting about someone's hand to get the ball rolling, so it's always going to be different depending on the person. The cool thing is that if you're actually looking at person's hand looking for these things,then you're taking an interest and you're halfway there, simply practicing your hobby, something you're interested in. The attention is deflected to their hands, and instead of gawping at someone wondering what to say to them your focus is elsewhere. Staring at a beautiful woman for too long can be extremely off-putting for everyone concerned, so I suggest you avoid making it a habit and instead learn to focus on their hands and other aspects of their personality. Beautiful women get stared at all the time, but rarely have their palm read. Be interested in the person, not their looks, and you'll both feel a lot more comfortable.

The Real World

The truth is, nothing can prepare you for doing this stuff 'for real'. Lines are hard to read, people aren't that forthcoming with information, it can be hard to hear what people are saying in loud environments and you can be interrupted or lose your flow. The only way to get good at readings is to practice, but here are some things you should consider before you rush off and attempt a palm reading.

Questions Questions

I know I've said before that what you're giving is more akin to a personality reading than 'fortune telling', but some people have their own ideas and will come right out and ask you questions about their future. The bulk of these questions will be concerning relationships, either ones they're in or are yet to have. I strongly advise against giving ANY type of advice, especially in the context of this book. The most you can do is help the person reflect on their personality reading and use this, with their help, to figure out whether they're doing the right thing or heading in the right direction in their lives. If you use your common sense you'll simply be agreeing with people; with cautious people to be cautious, or with people desperate for change that change might be good for them. Have a conversation and let the person answer their own questions by asking them more questions.

MEGA TOP TIP: Don't give advice, ever. Let people answer their own questions.

Availability

Questions are often about relationships and can reveal the romantic status of the person whose hand you are reading. In most cases you'll know pretty quickly whether someone has a boyfriend or not. While you're giving a reading, you'll often hear people say 'That's just like my boyfriend' or 'That's what my boyfriend is always saying' not just because it's true, but because the person wants to get across that they're romantically unavailable. It could also be because they're looking out for their single friends and may want to point you in their direction.

Friends

No matter how long you spend giving a reading, people are usually left wanting to know more about themselves, making it hard not to end on a downer. A good way to stop this happening, and to get even more attention, is to bring the subject around to best friends.

Girls like to see what their best friend's hands reveal about them so they can compare notes. You'd be amazed how people open up when there's a close friend to join in with, and if you give a reading to a group of friends the others will look on with interest, joining in with knowing glances, winks and 'told you so' looks. Friends tend to 'gang up' on each other when they're having a reading as it's a good excuse to tease each other, so when you're in this situation you'll find you can be more cheeky and take a few more 'cheeky' risks with your reading than normal. Anything you say that a person disagrees with is often greeted with a chorus of approval and laughter from their friends. Take advantage of these situations and have some fun.

Boyfriends

'Boyfriend compatibility' questions are one thing, giving someone's boyfriend a reading is another. It's your call whether you give a guy a reading while his girlfriend watches or not, and although you may be able to have great fun doing this you need to decide whether the boyfriend in question is receptive. My advice is to tread lightly; not all boyfriends are up for it. You may not be trying to pass yourself off as a professional palm reader, yet if a girl tries to get you to read her boyfriend's palm he will probably assume you do it for a living. Make sure you're honest in these situations, and whatever you do try not to make fun of him. They don't like that. In fact, try to make him look good, and see if there's anything genuinely amusing you can say to regarding his behaviour as it pertains to his girlfriend. You might get some laughs out of it, and winning over a boyfriend can make you seem less of a threat to a group. Just don't let yourself get turned into a performing monkey, and if the boyfriend and his friends seem even remotely hostile you're probably better off out of there.

Another thing you can offer to do for a boyfriend is take a look at his handwriting, something guys tend to find more interesting than palmistry as it sounds more scientific and believable, and less touchy-feely or 'girly'. You'll learn how useful it is to have another skill like graphology for different situations later in this book.

Palmistry On A Date

Let's not forget that when you are giving a reading and you are actually on a date, there's a good chance that the other person will want to know more about YOU. Well, you'd hope so wouldn't you? In that case you're going to have to be willing to give yourself a reading or at least talk about your own hand, which hopefully you will have prepared in advance.

Comparing readings is great, in fact you could argue that if you've got to the stage where someone else is interested in you enough to want to compare palms or handwriting then you're actually getting somewhere. What would be really nice is for both your palm readings to be compatible. Luckily as you're the one giving the readings you can make them as compatible as you like!

One thing you must bear in mind is not to make things overly compatible. If you're too eager and describe everything you see on your hand as being incredibly similar and complementary to someone else's hand you can come across as a bit creepy. Don't be afraid to point out the differences too as it can be good fun and sometimes quite funny. You can make up some crazy stuff as you're going and don't be afraid to make fun of yourself.

Above all, be yourself and don't mirror someone else's personality too much. People like differences as much as similarities; 'complimentary' can apply to opposites too.

Examples

- 'My heart line is quite a bit longer than yours, which means I've been known to cry watching soppy films while you'd prefer to watch Terminator 2.'

- 'Your head line shows that you're a bit of a worrier, and you have a tendency to overthink things. My head line is really short, which means I'll never understand why you overthink things.'

- 'Your palm is very soft. Feel mine, it's rugged and tough like a man. However this line shows that I'm useless at putting up a shelf.'

- 'You have long fingers like mine, which shows that we're both creative. We'd probably argue a lot about our favourite TV shows and what music to listen to.'

Similar to when we discussed the need for having a backstory for each skill, you really need to know what your own hand says about your particular personality. Not only is creating a palm reading for yourself good practice, it'll give you the confidence you need to show your compatibility with someone else at a moments notice. You've got all the time in the world to make your own palm reading interesting and funny so spend the time on it and you'll never be caught out.

Too Much Information

Hopefully by this point you will have grasped the idea that for our purposes, giving a reading is mostly about process and little to do with 'facts'. We're learning to 'talk the talk' with as little information as possible so we can focus on getting our mouths in gear and spend less time fretting that we 'don't know enough'. A common mistake many novice readers make is to learn and internalise so many meanings of things before they start that they close down the moment they are confronted with a real situation. The last thing you want is to clam up the moment someone shows you their palm; with less information to remember you'll be less likely to stare into space and more likely to get a conversation started.

Time for another analogy, this time about bicycles.

Learning to ride a bicycle is all about technique, and studying how the wheels of a bike work won't stop you from falling off during your first few attempts. Cycling is a practical pursuit; getting bogged down in the technicalities will prevent you from riding!

It's similar with readings. The more readings you attempt the more that the literature on the subject will make sense, but without any real-world experience you'll have no frame of reference. Sure, books can help you hone your technique once you've had a few outings, but at some point you'll need to take a leap of faith and get on the bike or you'll never get anywhere.

Give readings whenever you can, and learn from your mistakes; only by falling off can you learn to ride. Getting on the bike repeatedly is the only way forward, take off your stabilisers by leaving the manual behind often. If you're not wobbling, you're not learning.

Go forth and wobble. Call it a swagger.

Putting It All Together

Let's bring the information from the lines and the fingers together for the first time and look at another example. This time, we'll look at hand with a short straight heart line, that doesn't touch a short head line that curves towards the wrist and a long life line that starts somewhere close to the first finger, with a strong first finger that some of the other fingers bend towards.

Lines

- Short heart line runs straight across palm = Less expressive / Sensitive and needy / Emotionally closed / Loner

- Heart and head line not touching = nothing

- Short head line that curves towards the wrist = creative, quick thinker

- Long life line that starts near the first finger = energetic and ambitious

Fingers

- 1st Finger long, strong and unbending = ambitious

- 2nd Finger bends towards 1st finger = responsibility leaning towards ambition

- 3rd Finger bends towards 2nd finger = creativity leaning towards responsibility (and ambition)

- 4th Finger normal / straight = communication not a problem

You can see that having the fingers as well as the lines gives us more to talk about. Although you'll be talking about each line and then each finger in order before you give your overall impressions, looking at a list of traits like this can show you quite clearly how some traits compliment each other and others contradict each other:

Let's put all these traits into one long list to take a look at which things compliment and contradict each other:

- Less expressive / Sensitive and needy / Emotionally closed / Loner

- Impulsive

- Creative, quick thinker

- Energetic and ambitious

- Ambitious (again)

- Responsibility leaning towards ambition

- Creativity leaning towards responsibility

- Communication not a problem

As you can see by now, combining the lines with the meanings of the fingers gives us a huge amount of information. If you were to simply recite these meanings to someone the reading would be incredibly static and boring, but like before we're going to compare contrasting traits to fuel the conversation.

Before I give an example reading, let's look at the two conflicting sides of this hand's traits:

A: There's a lot of ambition here, a short head line showing a creative, quick thinker, a long life line that starts near the first finger **and** a strong first finger that the other fingers tend to bend towards.

Summary: Ambition / Creative / Quick Thinking

B: Somewhat contrary to that we have a short heart line that runs straight across the palm showing a sensitive and needy person who is rather emotionally closed, and who appears to forsake responsibility and perhaps creativity in the pursuit of ambition.

Summary: Sensitive / Needy / Emotionally closed

Of course in the real world we won't take this long overview before we start; we'll just plunge straight in with the heart line and take it from there. Here's an example reading that brings everything together.

Verbal Example

'So you have quite an interesting hand here, let's take a look. So do you know anything about palmistry? Well this is the heart line, and it runs here from the side of the hand across your palm underneath your fingers. I must admit, I've seen longer heart lines but don't worry, it doesn't mean you're heartless! It could mean that you're slightly more reserved than most people. I'm not sure if that makes much sense, so can we just look at the other lines to see what we can see?[PAUSE]

'It's funny, your head line is this one here, and although it's quite short too did you know that a short head line actually means a quick thinker? Instead of taking forever thinking things through, there's a chance you can be quite impulsive at times.[PAUSE]

'Also you'll see the head line is bending down towards your wrist. Are you creative at all?[PAUSE]

'Ok, so you have a job that you hate, but I guess yes, you should get back on to writing that book you've started and stopped a few times! There's definitely a creative streak here. And you know what? That could be what that short heart line is all about; you need time alone to do your thing.[PAUSE]

'So this is your life line but don't worry, I can't tell how long you're going to live. But you do have this big long curving life line which shows you certainly have enough energy to throw into things once you put your mind to it.[PAUSE]

'Actually, that ties in quite nicely with the next thing, your fingers. Did you know that your fingers also tell a story too? Well they do, and in fact your forefinger here, your pointing finger, is quite strong, and all these other fingers seems to be bending towards it. Your pointing finger is all about getting what you want and knowing where to go in life, and I'd say that this finger is definitely the strongest one of the fingers on your hand. I take it you can be quite stubborn?[PAUSE]

'That's interesting, because although you know what you want and part of you isn't that scared of getting it, I do feel that perhaps that, if anything, it's the introverted streak I noticed in your heart line holding you back a bit.[PAUSE]

'So let's take a look at these other fingers. This one next to your index finger is all about responsibility, and like the next one along, the creativity finger, both of them are leaning somewhat towards your stronger pointing finger. In palmistry, it's said that fingers that lean against others are relying on them for strength.[PAUSE]

'Yes that's right, your drive to succeed in whatever you do does come at a cost. I'm not saying you're irresponsible, or not creative as we've seen your creativity in your head line, but it could be that your single-mindedness can come at a price.[PAUSE]

'If you look here at your little finger you'll see it really has nothing to do with the other fingers, it's out on a limb! The little finger is all about communication, a bit like if you pretend holding an imaginary telephone to your head and the finger is the mouthpiece. Yup, that's how I remember it too! Anyway, it seems you don't really have a problem with communication.[PAUSE]

'Yes, that does seem somewhat contradictory to this heart line of yours! I guess that's what makes you interesting, and what makes you able to write books. Some of the time you really need to be on your own, but you also have this massive outgoing streak which enables you to get what you want.[PAUSE]

'So people say there's two sides to every person, and I think that's reflected in your hand. What do you think?[PAUSE]

'Cool. Thanks for showing me your hand, to be honest I'm not really sure about this stuff but I'd like to hear more about that book of yours…'

A few notes about this example:

- Try to avoid negativity, especially at the start of a reading. I could've easily simply reeled off the meaning of a short heart line, but to be honest that would have been just rude. Give yourself time to think, you're trying to build people up, not assassinate their character!

- People will try and make sense of what you are saying by attaching it to their own lives and current predicament. Here we have someone who is quick to point out that they are unhappy with their job, and see the creative streak shown on their hand as their idea of writing a novel. Join in, and follow their lead.

- Just because the reading has wound down doesn't mean the conversation is over. Keep it going; hopefully you'll know enough about the person to keep chatting and find out more about them.

Graphology

Some of the material in this chapter is taken from my book 'Graphology - The Art Of Handwriting Analysis'

By this point you should have a fair idea of how to put a short palmistry reading together and understand the mechanics of how a reading can work. The graphology system you'll learn in these pages is designed to be extremely simple and fun to remember, so if you've got even half a handle on palmistry you should find graphology a breeze; no one will be expecting you to tell them their fortune and it's a whole lot less intimidating than holding someone's hand. You'll also find it ideal for situations where palmistry just doesn't feel right. Graphology is a lot more hands off than palmistry, quite literally.

It's rare to meet anyone that's ever had their handwriting analysed, so you'll find that people are quite receptive as it has a high novelty factor. Unlike palmistry, it's easy to interpret a group of people's handwriting simultaneously, telling people the things they should be looking out for as you go. As the different elements are easy to spot (when you've told people what to look for), people can compare each other's scribbles as you point out the similarities and differences between each person's scrawl as you go. It's a lot easier for people to compare their handwriting than their palms so you'll find that once you've told a group of people just a few of the things to look out for they'll be comparing each other's handwriting almost immediately without any prompting on your part.

The Typical Female

This system only needs the word 'typical' to be written down, plus a person's signature. Everyone likes to think they're unique, but you're going to be asking people if they think they're a typical female. This is not only quite amusing, but the word 'typical' contains the letters T, Y, P and I which are some of the most useful letters in graphology. By asking people 'Are you a typical female?' you will have quite a lot of information to work with. Nobody likes to think that they're typical in the slightest, so talking about 'the typical female' will usually cause a fair amount of amusement.

Having people write the word 'typical' plus their normal signature is fine for when you're short on paper in an impromptu situation, such as writing on the back of a bar receipt if you're in a pub or club. If possible, it's more fun to get people to write the entire sentence 'I am a typical female' which they then sign as if it were some kind of formal declaration. With a group of people this can be great fun as they'll tend to hide their handwriting from each other as if it were some kind of test. Whether you try this with a handful of people or use it one-on-one, the 'typical female' story has a lot of mileage as it's light-hearted and tongue in cheek.

First we're going to look at the letters T and I together using something I call 'The Golf Analogy'. The letters T and I tell us about the person's general demeanour and this analogy will help us remember these letter meanings while giving us a fun way to interpret them. We'll then look at the letters Y and P, which can tell us a something about how sociable and physical a person is. These meanings all adhere to the ideas of traditional graphology so even though you'll be interpreting them in a somewhat simplified form you won't be caught out by someone who has studied graphology in any depth. Once again this is the real-deal, simplified.

The Letters T & I - The Golf Analogy

By using The Golf Analogy with the letter T and the letter I in the word 'typical' the whole word becomes the fairway / golf course.

Imagine that the letter T represents the golfer and the crossing of the T represents his swing (easily remembered as this is the Tee Shot)

Imagine that the stem of the letter I represents the flag on the golfing green where the hole is.

Imagine that the dot of the I represents the golf ball.

The way someone swings at the ball can tell us something about the way the person approaches life, and her accuracy in getting the ball near the hole (flag) shows us something about her ability to reach her goals.

Does she aim ridiculously high and overshoot? Or take a small but direct shot and get a hole in one? Does the ball miss the mark even though she hit the ball with great strength, or does it land very close to the flag against all odds after having been driven into the ground?

Examples

What can we say about this person in our imaginary game of golf?

From this handwriting sample, we can see a high and hard swing has overshot the hole considerably. This is likely to be someone who has a great deal of enthusiasm but often over-stretches herself.

This person on the other hand has taken a perfectly measured and straight shot and landed right on the flag. This denotes a person who takes quick decisive action and pays attention to detail.

This person has managed to get the ball on the flag even though she's driven it into the fairway. Probably someone who doesn't look too far ahead and doesn't have wild ambition, but gets what she wants eventually.

As you can see with these three examples, you can get quite a lot out of this analogy and it's great fun.

The Height Of The Dot

It is perfectly possible to have the dot of the I directly above the stem but still at some distance (height) from the main letter.

This still constitutes a 'hit' or 'hole in one' - however, the higher the dot is from the stem, the less the person is satisfied with their success and will still be yearning for higher things and further achievements.

If there is no dot on the I at all we can assume that the ball is missing in the rough - the person is somewhat confused about where to put their energy and isn't quite sure where their goals lie!

IN A NUTSHELL

The way someone plays golf in our imaginary game of Ts and Is shows us how they approach life

The swing is the crossing of the T, the I is the flag and the dot of the I is the ball

The Letters Y and P - Sociability And Physicality

The letters Y and P both have a curved or looped shape when written in lower case. Some people draw large loops, some draw small loops and some people hardly draw loops at all. The bigger the loop the more of that letter's trait someone has.

The size of the loop in the letter Y shows us how gregarious and sociable someone is. Think 'You' for the Y, the bigger the loop the more open the person. The size of the loop in the letter P shows us how physical someone is. Think 'Physical' for the P, the bigger the loop the more physical the person.

Taking these two letters together enables us to come to some conclusions.

Small Y loop / large P loop - Socially selective, could make up for it with physical activity
Large Y loop / small P loop - Gregarious, may prefer to spend time socially rather than in physical activity
Small Y loop / small P loop - Socially selective, not that physical, tends to be a loner
Large Y loop / large P loop - Gregarious and physically active, probably enjoys team sports and social outings

If the loops are so tight that there is hardly any loop to them at all this can denote a shyer quieter type.

Comparing the size of the loops of the letters Y and P can give you a lot of mileage and when you combine this with the letters T and I in the golf analogy you have quite a lot to compare. However one should not only judge the loops against each other but also against the size of the overall writing. If the loops are incomplete or end abruptly this can indicate frustration socially and/or physically.

IN A NUTSHELL

Y loops show how much 'you' i.e. themselves people project into the world
P loops shows how physical people are

Bigger loops - more
Smaller loops - less

TOP TIP: If you are having problem judging the loops or there simply aren't any at all, judge and compare the length of the stems from the Y and the P.

Slants And Baselines

The slants and angles that people display in their handwriting shows us their slants and angles on life. People's handwriting tends to slant either forwards or backwards, and when they write a sentence on unlined paper the handwriting will rise or fall across the page (called the baseline). The meanings of these tendencies are fairly self-explanatory and easy to remember.

Slants

The slant of someone's handwriting refers to the way the letters in a word appear to be leaning to the left or right. Most people's handwriting tends to lean somewhere between being perfectly upright or leaning slightly forward:

The more that the handwriting slants forwards and to the right, the more emotionally responsive someone is said to be:

The more that the handwriting slants backwards and to the left, the more emotionally withdrawn someone is said to be:

People who lean towards you when you talking are emotionally involved and interested in what you are saying - people who lean away from you are far more guarded and withdrawn.

Top Tip: It is very rare that someone's handwriting slants both to the left AND to the right over the course of a sentence or phrase. However, if you do see this rare occurrence it is seen to represent someone with a dual personality.

Baselines

Working out if a person's handwriting rises or falls across the page is extremely easy to spot in most cases, but if you are having trouble then it is a simple matter to imagine that the paper is lined horizontally and judge the handwriting from there. Someone whose writing rises up the page has an upbeat optimistic character, and when the writing falls down the page they have a more pessimistic downbeat view of the world.

Straight baseline - Normal

Rising baseline - Upbeat

Falling baseline - Downbeat

Someone who has a wavy or uneven baseline could be rather up and down as you can imagine!

TOP TIP: Watch out for left handed people! They write differently, so pay attention to which hand people use.

IN A NUTSHELL

Handwriting slants forward = they lean towards you i.e. they are open and sociable
Handwriting slants backward = they lean away from you i.e. they are somewhat reserved

Handwriting rises up the page = the person is optimistic
Handwriting falls down the page = the person is pessimistic

Signature

The signature of a person is their most personal scribble. Just like when we analysed the word 'typical', the slant and baseline concepts all apply and it's rare to find a signature that doesn't reflect someone's overall handwriting style in some way.

What They Write

The personal information someone reveals in their signature can be quite telling. To begin with, simply ignore the style of signature completely and see if they've used all their names, initials or a bit of both.

Someone who writes their full name is usually a person who is steadfast and trustworthy:

Someone who misses out their first name by using an initial is more formal and less open about themselves:

A signature that is simply someone's first name shows someone who is very open and informal, even flamboyant:

A surname only can show seriousness:

This is largely common sense. A signature shows how someone projects themselves to the outside world and the way they use their first names or surnames reflects that.

TOP TIP: As mentioned in the previous section, always remember that the person is connected to their hand and signature; the way they write it, the way they use a pen, their entire attitude should be taken into consideration when judging their handwriting. You're not analysing people's handwriting by post or email, you're engaging with the person face to face on a personal level so don't forget to use your common sense and natural intuition.

Style

The style in which someone actually writes their signature can also tell us a fair bit about them. As before, the rise or fall of a signature up and down the page can denote a positive or pessimistic attitude to life. However there are two more things to consider:

Can you read it? - An illegible signature can show egotism. However, it can also be that of someone who signs their signature a lot.

Is it underlined? - An underlined signature can show a powerful character:

A full stop at the end can also show assertion. People who write full stops at the end of their signatures can be quite powerful characters, although set in their ways.

If there is a huge difference between someone's general writing style and the style of their signature you have the makings of an interesting analysis there is obviously some kind of inner conflict going on with the individual.

IN A NUTSHELL

The way the person writes their first and last names show you how they project themselves

The style of a person's signature, although open for interpretation, can be somewhat telling

TOP TIP: Signatures have a personality of their own, somewhat like art. Take a look at as many signatures as you can and try to imagine what each person is like, based solely on their handwriting style. You'll be surprised the conclusions you come to, even without using the techniques in this book.

Putting It All Together

By interpreting the four letters T,Y,P and I along with a signature we can get an idea of how a person approaches life, see how outgoing and physical they are and get a handle on their overall personality. Just as we did with palmistry, we can look for compliments and contradictions between the traits to generate discussion. We will comment on each of the traits one by one, leaving pauses to see if we're on the right track and to encourage conversation, before bringing all the traits together at the end for an overview.

Here's an example:

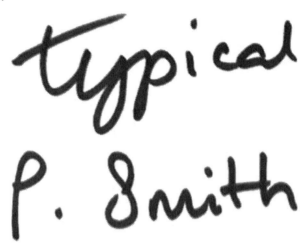

- Long upwards T shot, dot of the i somewhat to the right and a bit high
- Large Y and small P
- Leaning forwards, sloping upwards
- Signature first letter of first name, second name (formal, a bit cold)

Looking a the word 'typical' and using the golf analogy, we can see that the crossing of the T is very high and very long, showing someone who aims high with a lot of ambition; this is definitely an enthusiastic person. We can also see that the dot of the I is somewhat high and not exactly over the letter itself. Putting this together, we have someone who may overstretch themselves and not always reach all their goals, though not from lack of trying and effort.

We can see from the large loop in the Y someone who is quite sociable, but from the lack of loop in the P a person who is not quite so physical. The whole word is slanted forward, which compliments the sociable Y, and it's rising up the page, denoting an upbeat and positive nature. This all compliments what has gone before.

Interestingly, this person's signature seems somewhat at odds with their previous writing of the word 'typical'. They've only written an initial for their first name, yet they've underlined their surname. It appears to be that rather than being sociable and open, this signature is written by someone who is quite formal and likes to present a powerful image of themselves.

Verbal Example

So what can we say about this entire handwriting sample? If you've worked through and understood the palmistry section you'll know that the friction between the word 'typical' and signature is a a contradictory goldmine. Here's an example reading one could give, with the comparisons and contradictions emboldened as before, with pauses inserted to give the other person, and yourself, time to think and converse.

'We can see here from the letter T you have crossed it with a very long upwards stroke. This is a sign of someone who is positive, outgoing and is somewhat ambitious. If you think of crossing of the letter T a bit like someone taking a swing at a golf ball, this shot would be aiming high and into the distance, don't you think? [PAUSE]

'If we look at the dot of the letter I, we can see where the ball actually ended up. As you can see, the dot of your I is also very high, but not exactly over the letter I itself. If you imagine that the letter I is the flag where the hole is, you've overshot it somewhat! I'd imagine that you are very enthusiastic and put a lot of energy into things, but perhaps you either try and do too much and aim too high? I'm not saying you never reach your goals, but perhaps you could reduce the amount you do and concentrate on the big stuff? [PAUSE]

'Let's take a look at the letter P and the letter Y. What we're looking for here are the loops of the letters. You see here, your letter Y has a very large loop. It's pretty easy to remember what the letter Y means, it's all about YOU. How you present yourself to the world, how outgoing you are, that kind of thing. So this large loop in the letter Y would suggest that you're a very outgoing person, pretty sociable. [PAUSE]

'If we look at the loop of the letter P, the letter P is all about physicality. The more of a loop you have the more physical you are. Now you have a letter P with no visible loop whatsoever! Would you agree that you're more sociable than physical? I'm not saying you never do any exercise, I'm just wondering if this makes any sense? [PAUSE]

'You think you're pretty active? OK, well that's interesting anyway, you quite like sports and are fairly physical, perhaps we'll find out what that P is all about later! If we look at the way you've written the word 'typical' we can see that it's sloping upwards and is leaning forwards, all traits of a positive upbeat kind of person. So that's the word 'typical', lets take a look at your signature shall we?

'So your signature is interesting as you've written your surname in full but not your first name, do you always write it like that? [PAUSE]

'Usually people who don't write their first names are a little bit formal, not exactly shy, but they don't like to give too much away about themselves. [PAUSE]

'And here, you've written your surname in full and you've underlined it to make a point. That is the sign of a strong woman! Perhaps you've had to fight for what you want when it comes to work, or you have to put a formal face on when you do business? [PAUSE]

'So this is interesting, although you're outgoing and highly sociable, you have this slight distance you put between yourself and others. [PAUSE]

'So although we're trying to see if you're a typical female, you have this high drive to achieve and appear to have the demeanour to go through with it all. I'm still confused about this physical P loop though. Have you had any injuries in the past? [PAUSE]

'It's strange because sometimes people's handwriting changes as they evolve, sometimes it can even reflect their lives. Perhaps you need to stop working so much and give yourself more time to follow the sports and activities you enjoy, it could show a sign of frustration.[PAUSE]'

There are fewer contradictions in this graphology reading than in the palmistry reading example, but it does show that a reading of this nature can still go on for quite some time. Different methods have different rhythms, so it's interesting to see how the shape and feel of a reading changes considerably simply because the focus is on someone's handwriting and not their palm. Palmistry readings feel 'intimate', graphology readings feel a lot more 'open'. It's hard to explain, but you'll get a feel for it once you get out there and put this stuff into practice.

You can see that I've underlined a couple of sections in the last example, mainly to show what can happen when someone's handwriting is telling you one thing, yet it's plainly obvious that it's less than accurate or applicable. In this case, the person has no loop on the letter P, yet she is quite obviously fairly sporty and physical. If this happens there is no need to panic; the handwriting is telling you one thing, the person another! What you need to do is keep calm, and attempt to get to the bottom of it. Perhaps you will, perhaps you won't. In this example I decided, with the help of the person in question, that perhaps the 'no loop P' meant that she should spend less time working and more time with her physical activities; in effect, this P showed a frustration in her life.

TOP TIP: Don't panic about being wrong. If a trait shows you one thing yet the person disagrees with it, try to get to the bottom of it, together. Use the other traits to try and 'solve the mystery' with their help. It's fun, and like contradictions, 'misses' brings a lot of colour to your readings and get the other person involved on a deeper level. If you can learn to love irregularities, mismatches and friction you'll never, ever be phased.

The Approach

You'll find that giving a graphology reading is less involved than giving a palm reading, as once you point out a specific trait (such as a high 'T shot' for instance) it will not be forgotten due to its more visual and immediate nature; it's in plain sight for all to see. Because of this, graphology is less abstract to the layperson than palmistry. Combine the two, however, and you have yet another source of comparisons and contradictions.

Unlike palmistry where you need to take in interest in someone's hands to grab their attention, graphology isn't quite as immediate simply because you need a pen and paper to get started. As our mobile phones have all but replaced pen and paper these days, it would be pretty strange to produce a writing implement from your pocket. Luckily in most social situations there is a scrap of paper floating about in the form of a receipt, beer mat or napkin, and bar staff are usually happy to furnish you with a pen if you ask nicely.

My favourite way to introduce graphology is after giving someone a palm reading, but that isn't always going to be possible and there will be moments when graphology is far more appropriate than palmistry; you simply need to look out for opportunities. In some places people are still required to sign for their purchases, and although it would be creepy to hover around someone who is signing their bar tab, you can still use these moments to your advantage. With palmistry you notice someone's hands, with graphology you can notice someone's handwriting.

Regarding getting someone's attention, it would look kind of strange if you were studying your own hand at a bar. However, doodling around with your own handwriting is relatively normal; we've all tried different ways of writing our signatures on occasion. Being deep in thought, trying out different ways of writing your signature shouldn't appear that strange, especially if you've recently read somewhere that you can change the course of your life by changing your signature. You'll need a second opinion, of course. By casually asking someone which signature they prefer out of two or three of your own attempts you can get a conversation going with someone, before asking them if they think they're a typical female and have they heard of the 'typical female' test...

Once you have even a passing knowledge of the graphology presented here, you'll notice all kinds of situations where it's appropriate. You just have to look out for them, and work with the moment. I'll reiterate once again that you're not putting yourself out there as a graphology ninja, you're just a guy who's interested in people and who has learnt a thing or two about handwriting on his travels. As always; keep it light, but do it right.

TOP TIP: You can always carry a pen or pencil around with you, just be sure not to suddenly produce it as if you were 'ready' for a graphology reading as that would look very strange indeed. More spontaneous is to go and 'find' a pen or pencil, but bring back yours. A small golf pencil can fit in your back pocket and won't leak. In fact, 'finding' a pencil (on the floor, for instance) could lead to a reading. Even though you've had it on you the whole time.

TOP TIP: Be careful not to creep single ladies out by asking them this kind of stuff as they'll quite often (rightly) assume the whole thing is simply a chat up ploy. Ladies in pairs or groups will feel far less threatened and as you're 'outnumbered' they'll probably enjoy telling you how terrible your signature is. Setting yourself up for some friendly derision can work very well.

Numerology

Some of the material in this chapter is taken from my books 'Numerology - Numbers Past And Present With The Lo Shu Square' and Cartomancy - Fortune Telling With Playing Cards

Although people often choose numbers and dates in their lives that they believe bring the most luck, numerology readings normally focus on the one number that can't be changed in a person's life; their birth date. Numerology based on people's birthdays is similar to the personality readings we've already discussed in this book, so instead of using the numbers from a person's birth date we're going to look at a number very much more current than the day they were born; their mobile phone number.

There are a few reasons for this. For one it's different, and different is good. You're far more likely to kick off a conversation about 'phone number readings' simply because it's so unusual. A person's mobile phone number is the holy grail of contact details and if you've obtained it in the first few minutes of meeting someone you should be quite pleased with yourself. Secondly, it gives you a chance to talk about the recent past, the present and the near future by using a number that is used on a daily basis. And last but not least, it's a lot less forward and potentially embarrassing than asking people for their date of birth. If you're in your twenties this shouldn't be a problem but for ladies in their thirties and beyond, revealing one's age to a complete stranger can be a bit much to ask.

To give any kind of numerology reading you're going to have to learn the meanings of the numbers one to nine. Nine meanings for nine numbers can appear quite daunting for some people, but if you follow through my descriptions in the next chapter you should be up to speed in no time.

Number Meanings

To help us to get 'visual' with our numbers and to connect as much meaning to them as possible we can use a 'life cycle' story that makes sense through the numbers one to ten. When we see a number we need a whole array of ideas, concepts and images to come to mind and by getting creative with our visualising we can actually learn, with a little practice, what each of the numbers mean without too much fuss.

Here are the basic meanings of the numbers one to ten:

1. Beginnings

2. Cooperation

3. Expansion

4. Security

5. Activity

6. Communication

7. Spirituality

8. Inspiration

9. Changes

10. Success

The numbers one to ten go through a cycle and the 10 at the end is in many ways similar to the 1 at the start; the 10 is the realisation of all that the 1 can be. If you think of all the numbers going around in a big circle starting and ending with the number one on a clock you get the idea; the ten becomes a one again and the cycle repeats. This is analogous to the 'life cycle' that we all go through.

The Life Cycle

Think about this little story for a moment:

- We all begin alone, we couple up, and bring life into the world, before we make a home with four walls.

- There is much activity as the child grows, and before long the child learns to communicate, and asks big questions about the world around him.

- Finally he is inspired to go out into the world, make a difference, and be successful.

- He's now alone, and the cycle can begin again.

Here it is again with each number and meaning at the relevant point in the story progression:

- We all begin alone (1: Beginnings) we couple up (2: Cooperation) and bring life into the world (3: Expansion) before we make a home with four walls (4: Security).

- There is much activity as the child grows (5: Activity) and before long the child learns to communicate (6: Communication) and asks big questions about the world around him (7: Spirituality).

- Finally he is inspired to go out into the world (8: Inspiration) make a difference (9: Changes) and be successful (10: Success).

- He's now alone (1: Beginnings) and the cycle can begin again.

By thinking of the numbers in this way it also gives us the feeling of progression; higher numbers are the end of the cycle and lower numbers the start of the cycle.

Let's go through that story again in greater detail. This whole story is designed so that you can remember the meanings of the numbers quickly and easily.

1 The Power Of One - I Stand Alone - Beginnings

We have to start somewhere, and with a blank canvas there is a lot of energy and optimism. We could be starting from scratch, or starting again (coming full circle). We're number one! There's no fear and anything's possible. This number one isn't about knowing you've arrived; it's about knowing you could get there if you put your mind to it. It's the optimism and naivety of a teenager who's willing to try anything and is free from old habits or preconceived notions. This number one is selfish, but's it's a healthy selfish; not the kind that crushes other people but drags others along with it's sheer optimism and idealistic outlook. Powerful stuff! However this boundless energy can be lacking in direction somewhat and needs focus to be truly effective.

Memory Tip: The number 1 looks like a capital I

2 Me And You - Two's Company - Cooperation

We don't stay alone and single forever. We meet someone, fall in love and in many ways our ego takes a step back as we learn to care for someone else. We learn to share, we learn to cooperate and do things together as a team. It's not always easy but it brings great rewards. We get to see the world another way, and we also learn to see things from another point of view. We form partnerships not just in our personal lives but our professional lives too.

Memory Tip: A number 2 looking in the mirror to it's left creates a heart shape. You can also imagine this as two swans coming together to create a heart silhouette

3 We Create Life - Three's a crowd - Expansion

Only two people can bring a third person into the world; it's how the human race has expanded to cover the entire globe. It's the growth of something from nothing, the fruits of cooperation. There can be labour pains, but the rewards are great. Let's not forget that even business partners often refer to their companies as 'babies'; the number three is all to do with seeing things come to life and grow beyond a mere concept.

Memory Tip: The number 3 looks like a pair of breasts to feed a baby

4 We Make A Home - These four walls - Security

When a child enters a couple's life they seek stability and the four walls of a place they can call 'home' for their family. Structure and order are required, safety and practicality. Although a lot needs to be done, there is a sense of settling down combined with achievement. For many people this is the end of a cycle for them as a happy home life with children is one of their life goals. Kids or not, the four represents the solid foundation required for future plans and growth.

Memory Tip: A square has four sides, like a simplistic house shape with square windows and doors

5 The Family Grows - Five alive - Activity

Once a baby becomes a child things get pretty hectic - a hive of activity! There's always something to do, plans to make, life is certainly never the same again. Life seems to go at twice the speed, everything seems to happen at once and multi-tasking is the order of the day. There is growth in so many ways, physically, mentally and socially, and sometimes it can feel out of control. One thing's for sure; you can't halt progress. This isn't like the number 3 which creates something from nothing; this is the growth of things that are already there.

Memory Tip: The number 5 looks like the handlebars and front wheel of a kids scooter which can remind you of the notion of speed and movement

6 The Child Learns To Communicate - Six is social - Communication

Before long the child is starting to communicate with the world around him and it's about personal interaction and a need to be understood. A child may attempt to communicate with sounds, looks and actions - even with his building blocks! The number six isn't just about phoning people up, it's about connecting with people too.

Memory Tip: The number 6 looks like an eye, or an ear, or a telephone

7 The Child Asks Big Questions - Seventh heaven - Spirituality

Once the child has learned to communicate he can start asking questions, and quite quickly they're questions we can hardly answer. 'Where did I come from?' is always a good one; it's funny how some of the first questions we ask as children are so difficult to answer! This need to understand and ask big questions has a spiritual ring to it. Where did we come from, how did we get here, what's it all about? The seven is all about looking up to the stars as we ask for some kind of divine inspiration.

Memory Tip: The number 7 looks like a question mark

8 The Child Is Inspired To Leave Home - Eight through the gate - Inspiration

The eight is when you leave home and do it for yourself, make your first strides towards independence and try out some of your own ideas for a change. You've got to get out there and make things happen, but it takes a leap of faith. You've got to believe you're ready for it but it takes inspiration and personal belief. It's almost like that lightbulb over the head moment where you 'get it' or have some flash of inspiration. But it's also about making the leap of faith required to make it happen.

Memory Tip: The number 8 looks like two 3's put together side on - the number 3 is the child, the number 8 being twice his size and ready to move on. 8 - lightbulb

9 He Makes A Difference - Plan Nine (From Outer Space) - Changes

You go out into the world and try to make a difference; you try and enable change. Unless things change you can very rarely get to where you want to go. Some of these changes will be changes you have to go through yourself, but many of them will be the changes which you've pushed through to reach your ultimate goal and there may well be sacrifices. When you can almost smell success you can't let anything get in your way and have to at times be ruthless. Nine is about nearly having it all. Don't give up; everything's going the right way.

Memory Tip: The number 9 is the activity before the success of 10/10. Like 6, the number 9 also looks like eye, ear, telephone but this time it's on a higher more adult level of communication and action fuelled by determination and knowledge

10 He Becomes Successful - Ten out of ten - Success

The child has realised his dreams and in many ways he has grown up. He has made a success of himself and achieved his ambitions. There is a sense of finality and accomplishment and the end of a cycle. The ten is for top marks, abundance and accomplishments earned through hard work and it took all the other stages to reach this point. With this sense of accomplishment can also come the sense of looking for pastures new; for another challenge. There can be a big difference between success and stability.

Memory Tip: Top marks, the realisation of a goal or dream. The end of a cycle and the start of a new one

This is just one way of looking at the numbers one to ten, but I wanted to explain the life cycle idea first because it's one of the simplest to remember. Some of the numbers are easier to grasp than others so here are some other things to bear in mind when you're trying to remember all of this:

1 and **10** are obviously beginnings and endings - the starts of things and everything that's exciting about new ventures, and the ends of things and the satisfaction of completion

2 for cooperation is pretty easy to remember, for love, balance, coming together

3 for expansion makes sense when you think of two people having a third to create a family - it's about concepts becoming reality and partnerships bearing fruit

4 for stability makes sense when you think of the four walls of a house - the family need somewhere to live, solid foundations

5 for the growth in the home itself, and the 'hive' of activity inside needing to expand outside of the four walls - it's the four walls of the house, with something growing inside of it!

6 for communication, the 6 looks like an eye, an ear AND a telephone!

7 for the spiritual 'seventh heaven' and the question- ing shape like a question mark

8 is 'out of the gate' - getting out there and doing it 9 is the final push for victory, the last mile, the planning coming to fruition

10 is the successful outcome, the realisation of every- thing that has gone before, the end of one cycle and the start of another

Let's remind ourselves of the whole story another way, this time dividing the numbers into three 'chapters' or sections:

1-3 : I Stand Alone / Two's Company / Three's A Crowd

The first three numbers are about fresh starts and early development

The numbers 1-3 have their own little story. A single person (1) meets someone (2) and has a baby (3). When you're a single young adult (1) it's all about excitement and trying new things out with great enthusiasm. Then you meet someone (2) and share your life with them in a less selfish way. Then (sometimes!) you have a baby (3) and you've both made a new number one!

These first three numbers are relatively easy to understand. I Stand Alone, Two's Company & Three's A Crowd are well known sayings and perfectly illustrate what each number means.

4-7 : These Four Walls / Five Alive / Six Is social / 7th Heaven

Numbers four to seven are more to do with childhood and the family growing

Security is needed so a house (4) is built for the family to live in. The baby grows into a child (5) and introduces all that crazy activity that revolves around having kids. The child learns to communicate and be- comes a true member of the family (6). As he becomes a young adult he asks more big questions and becomes more aware of his place in the world (7).

8-10 : Eight Through The Gate / Plan Nine / Ten Out Of Ten

These last numbers are more to do with adulthood and achievement

Finally the young adult leaves home to go and make his way in the world (8). He makes things happen, and his involvement in the real world shapes that world, even changes it (9). He becomes successful, realises his dreams and is able to stand on his own two feet (10). The moment this happens however the cycle is over and it is now HE who is the number one.

Phone Number Readings

So you now know a little about what the numbers one to nine mean, but how can we apply this to someone's mobile phone number to give them a reading?

Phone number readings are based on the idea that the numbers in a person's mobile phone number, usually a fairly new entry into their lives, could shed light on current events. So unlike palmistry or graphology readings, phone number readings are concerned with the recent past, the present and the near future. We can't escape the pre-ordained lines of the palm and our handwriting style develops until early adulthood, but the numbers that float in and out of our everyday lives are fairly random. Or are they? A phone number reading can help us find out.

Lucky Numbers

The idea of lucky numbers can lead fairly easily into the subject of numerology. Many people have a number they feel has followed them throughout their lives, and some people use the same 'lucky' numbers each and every time they do the lottery. For instance, the number 36 has turned up throughout my life more often than any other number (or so it seems), and for this reason I've always considered it my 'lucky number', although the wisdom in paying this number any attention has been the subject of much speculation! In any case, an easy way to prompt a numerology reading is to bring up the subject of lucky numbers as they're a safe bet and most people have one.

You don't need to be too clever about it, something like this is entirely appropriate:

"I'm terrible with numbers, but I've noticed that the number 36 has cropped up in my life more than any other number. Do you have a lucky number?"

You'll find that most people are happy to tell you their lucky number, but you should be aware that although some people's lucky numbers are based on happy events such as a wedding anniversary, they can also be derived from the birth dates of deceased loved ones. Don't assume that a person's lucky number is frivolous; you'll be surprised how many people take this stuff seriously and some people's numbers are chosen for extremely personal reasons.

Once you've ascertained a person's lucky number, or at least found a number that they consider to have appeared in their lives more often than most, you can switch your attention to their mobile phone number. You're going to have to write it down of course, and if you've been doing graphology already you're all set with a writing utensil and a piece of paper. If not, you're going to have to improvise.

The Number And The Prefix

Every mobile number has a prefix that is particular to a specific network. For instance, in the UK the prefix for the 02 network is 07595. We need not concern ourselves with those numbers as everyone on the network has them; what we're concerned with is the second half of the number that is unique to the individual. In the UK this is usually six digits. This may change in the future and may be different from country to country, but six digits is the norm in the UK at the time of writing this book.

In some circumstances you may find that the person has a brand new number having only recently changed provider. If that's the case, you can have a lot of fun comparing their old phone number with their new one. You'll find that some people know their mobile number off by heart, and other people can't actually remember it at all. This can tell you a lot about a person before you've even started; people's attitudes towards their mobile phone can be quite telling!

Bearing this in mind, it'll come as no surprise that people who know their number off by heart are sociable or often use their number for business, whereas people who have a new phone or use it very little won't have a clue. In fact, simply bringing up the topic of mobile phones usually gets people talking, blaming each other for either being on them the whole time or never answering them when they're called. A lot of people have mobiles but never even turn them on, unless they want to make a call.

Mobile phones; it's an age thing, a personality thing and a status thing all in one. You can tell a lot about someone from the state of their phone, what kind of cover they have, whether it's in the bottom of their handbag or in their hand constantly, whether it's even charged or switched on! As I've said before in these pages, use your common sense and read the obvious signs. Observe.

The Reading

So, you've talked to someone and ascertained their lucky number, and you now have their mobile number too. You're doing well! Here's how to turn these two numbers into a reading. As an example we're going to use someone who's got the mobile phone number **07595 326485**.

Firstly you write their phone number down **07595 326485**

Then you remove the network prefix, leaving you with **326485**. This is so you can get to the number that is more relevant to them, as everyone on the network will have the **07595** part.

Draw a line underneath this remaining number, and beneath it write their lucky number:

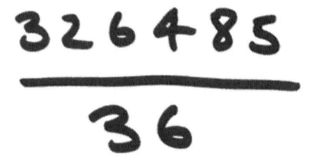

In the next stage you need to get to the 'base number' of each line of digits, by **repeatedly** adding the digits together until you are left with only one digit **OR** the number 10, as 10 has it's own meaning as we've already discussed when we looked at the number meanings.

For instance in the top six digit mobile number you add 3 + 2 + 6 + 4 + 8 + 5 = 28; you then add the 2 and the 8 together and are left with 10.

You do the same with their lucky number at the bottom if it's not a single digit already, so in this case we add the 3 and the 6 and arrive at 9. You **always** continue the addition until you are finished, which means you could end up with a string of fractions next to each other.

We've now ended up with this:

$$\frac{326485}{36} = \frac{28}{9} = \frac{10}{9}$$

Looking at the final result, the top digit 10 is their **Destiny Number** and is the number that shows the prevailing trend in their life at this time. The bottom digit 9 is their **Lucky Root** which shows a longer trend through their life, based on their own lucky number.

We now work out their **Number Of Opportunity** by taking the smaller number away from the bigger number (in this case, taking the Lucky Root 9 away from the Destiny Number 10). The number of opportunity is a number that they should look out for as they head into the future.

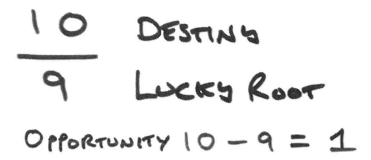

Destiny Number

The destiny number is derived solely from the original mobile phone number, and shows the prevailing trends in someone's current life. We know that the number 10 is all about success, so there's a current or possibility of success flowing through this person's life at the moment. The 10 is also the end of a cycle, so it may signify the end of an era for this person.

Lucky Root

The distilled version of the person's lucky number, their lucky root, is the number 9, which deals with changes at the end of a cycle. Perhaps if the person isn't feeling particularly blessed with luck over the last few years it's because she's still to achieve it? Or could it all be part of the destiny number 10 and the end of a cycle and the events leading up to it?

Number Of Opportunity

The number of opportunity is a number that the person should look out for to help her on her way. Her number is 1, all about new beginnings and fresh starts, so it could be that she needs to concentrate on wrapping up her current cycle so she can start afresh. Bearing the previous numbers in mind she definitely needs to look out for the 'next big thing' in her life.

As you can see, I've looked at these numbers in sequence, and tried to let each number answer each other's questions, similar to comparing lines of the hand or varying traits in someone's handwriting. The gold here is in looking for comparisons between the numbers and trying to figure out, with the help of the person whose numbers you are looking at, what it all means. As before you'll need to explain things as you go, leaving pauses for discussion.

Numbers are extremely abstract to most people and you'll need to explain the significance of each number in more detail than simply one word descriptions or the person simply won't be able to help you. However, as you criss-cross between the numbers during a reading, talking out loud and trying to make sense of everything together, you'll be able to come to some conclusions in a similar way to giving palmistry or graphology readings; the same rules apply. The ball is very much in the other person's court for most of the time so the more you can describe the meanings of each number the better.

Three numbers isn't that much to go on, and there will always be a need for more answers, so here are some other things you can look out for to answer questions and offer more clues.

Life Cycle

These readings cover the person's current life cycle up to the present day. You could argue that someone's current cycle started the day they got a new phone number, but generally it's better to look at the numbers as you go and let the person decide when it started and how each number fits into their current time frame. As a general rule it's best to treat the numbers to the left of the calculation as further back in time and the numbers to the right as more current. That way you can get a grip on when certain influences were taking place, especially useful when looking at resonant numbers.

Resonant Numbers

Resonant numbers are digits that repeat in your calculations and as such these numbers are seen to have special significance and influence all the others.

For instance, if we look at our entire calculation from beginning to end we can see that there are two 2s, two 3s, two 6s and two 9s.

$$\frac{326485}{36} = \frac{28}{9} = \frac{10}{9}$$

So these influences (resonances) are working in the background:

- 2 - Cooperation
- 3 - Expansion
- 6 - Communication
- 9 - Changes

The most obvious thing here is that we have two 9s, making it not only the person's lucky root but also a resonant number. This would show that there is even more focus on change, an undercurrent to the whole of this person's current cycle.

The resonant number 2 shows a background of cooperation, and also appears early on in our calculation, as well as mid-way through. This could indicate cooperation at different stages over the last few years, up until fairly recently. As mentioned before, you can use the idea of the calculation from left to right as a timeline to try and pinpoint when these resonances were at work.

The resonant 3, both which appear to the very left at the start of our calculation, represents expansion. This would indicate a lot of things going on at the start of this person's current cycle, new ventures and adventures. However, the number 3 doesn't appear anywhere else but the front, could this mean the adventure is over?

The resonant 6 shows communication, and both these 6s show early on in the calculation. Perhaps communication was important at the start of the person's current cycle, but has become less important as time has gone on. Perhaps communication has been lost in some way?

Absent Numbers

Numbers that don't appear at all in the calculation are considered 'absent', and unlike the opportunity number which is to be looked out for to make progress, absent numbers reflect on the ideas and energy that are missing from the person's current cycle and should be kept in mind for a more satisfying life. In our example there is no 7, and 7 is all to do with spirituality. Perhaps, if the person just slowed down a bit, she'd be happier with a little more downtime to reflect and think about the bigger picture. After all, there's been a lot going on, hasn't there? It's easy to forget what's important when you're busy.

Verbal Example

Here's an example of how this reading could pan out if it were to happen face to face. As before, you'll have to imagine this is a two way conversation, but it will help illustrate how a numerology reading of this type can feel.

'So we've added up all these numbers and we've arrived at these last two numbers. The number at the top, 10, is your destiny number, it shows the influences during your current life cycle, things that have happened over the last few years, that kind of thing. The number below it is your lucky root, the 9, this is a number that's been influencing you a lot longer and is a lot more personal.

'The number 10 is a pretty good number actually, it marks the end of a cycle. It's also a pretty successful number, like when you complete things, so there's been some good stuff happening too. Underlying all of that is this number 9, which has been influencing you a lot longer, and the number 9 is all about change. Do you feel like there's been a lot of change in your life over the last few years? [PAUSE]

'Ok, well when you take one of these numbers away from the other you get your opportunity number, this is a number you need to look out for in the future. If we take this 9 from this 10 we get 1, and the number 1 is as you'd imagine, all about new beginnings and fresh starts. Have you been thinking of doing anything new or going down a different path lately? [PAUSE]

'If we look at some of the numbers that repeat in all of this, we can see quite obviously that the number 9 repeats. Numbers that repeat are called resonant numbers, they work in the background and influence everything else. So this number 9 and the idea of change is working on more levels than just the obvious, and as they're at the end of all of this, on the right hand side, they're more recent changes that are working with you. [PAUSE]

'Going right to the front of our numbers, we can see two number 3s, so those have some influence too, probably at the start of this current cycle. So I'm thinking that recent developments started with a lot of expansion, 3 means expansion. [PAUSE]

'3 can also mean growth more than expansion, perhaps it's more about growth in general, a deeper kind of development. [PAUSE]

'You've also got two 2s and two 6s. Twos are about cooperation and 6s are about communication and very often these go hand in hand. Have you been involved in any joint ventures over the last few years, or been in a situation where other people had quite a lot of influence on you? [PAUSE]

'Well it could be your relationships, but as you've said, you've had a lot of pressure at work over the last few years. [PAUSE]

'Now it's kind of strange but there's only one number missing from all of this, and that's the number 7. When a number is missing from our lives we need to take a look at it to see if, quite literally, there's been something we're missing! The number 7 is all about spirituality, so I'm not sure if you're a spiritual kind of person or not, but what do you think? [PAUSE]

'Well I guess perhaps it's not just about spirituality, but more reflexive 'me' time. Perhaps it's telling you that you need to take the foot of the pedal a bit more if you're going to take advantage of any new beginnings.'

You'll see it's all quite general, each number contains quite a broad concept and there's a lot to think about. Let's not forget that you're simply reporting what the numbers mean using a system you've learned somewhere along the line, so you're not claiming to have great insight or know how to tell fortunes; you've picked up a bit of knowledge and it's fun to see how the numbers play out.

Unlike the palmistry and graphology methods outlined in this book, giving numerology readings like this does feel a bit more current as you're using something fairly recent such as a phone number, and although you're not making predictions, there's no harm in telling people to look out for a number here or there as long as you're not too specific.

The great thing about this system is that it's easy to do and remember and doesn't take up a huge amount of space on a piece of paper, yet by using the ideas of a destiny number, lucky root, number of opportunity, resonant numbers and absent numbers there are enough points of interest to play off each other while you're panning for gold.

Altogether Now

Even if you've got this far on a first read-through you should be well on the way to being, if nothing else, slightly more interesting to talk to.

Although there appears to be a lot of information in this book please never forget that its aim has been to equip you with just enough knowledge of palmistry, graphology and numerology to make your life a lot more fun and to enable you to create conversations out of thin air. So don't forget my bicycle analogy that cycling is a practical pursuit and getting bogged down in the technicalities will prevent you from riding. Get out there and try this stuff before you feel like an expert. On the whole people don't want experts, they want good conversations and fun times.

Don't wait till you think you know everything, get out there as soon as you think you know *something*. Play your knowledge down and avoid being labelled a guru. Gurus are weird, weird is on the verge of creepy, and creepy is **bad**. Be yourself; an interesting guy who's learnt some cool stuff.

Best get out there and kickstart some conversations!

Julian Moore

Bonus Chapter I - Star Signs

Some of the material in this chapter is taken from my book 'Star Signs - A Cool System For Remembering The Dates And Meanings Of The Twelve Signs Of The Zodiac'

You'd be hard pressed to meet anyone in the western world who didn't know their star sign and what it means. Knowing a little about astrology can go a long way, and it's especially fun to compare star signs for compatibility. Women in particular love comparing star signs between their friends. The only problem with star signs in general is that they're so common it's hard to claim it as a 'skill'. However, combined with everything else you'll learn in this book they can be pretty effective to get people talking. And we want to talk, right?

Knowing about star signs isn't that useful on its own, but when used in conjunction with everything else you've learned in this book it can become very handy. No matter what star sign someone has, they'll tend to agree with many of its associated traits and it's rare to meet someone who thinks that they're nothing like their sign at all.

Although it's out of the scope of this book to go into the meanings of each of the twelve signs of the zodiac, we'll now learn a simple method to remember the months that each star sign falls on that works about 87% of the time. You may overhear that it's someone's birthday, learn that someone was born in October or simply ask someone when they were born during the course of a reading. Either way you can use this knowledge to spice up your readings with a bit of knowledge that almost everyone can connect with.

Firstly I'll teach you a way to associate an image with each month of the year. Then, through a simple process of visualisation, to connect each month image with their star sign image, giving you the ability to know someone's star sign the moment you know their birthdate. Well, nine times out of ten anyway.

The Month Images

There are twelve months of the year and twelve signs of the zodiac. As we are going to be working with mental images we need to create a visualisation for each month so we can recall them instantly. As the months of the year are fairly abstract and don't actually 'look' like anything we can make them more stimulating by creating a mental image for each of them, such as the idea of Mayonnaise for the month of May.

Here are the twelve months of the year with their associated visualisations

- **January** - Jam

- **February** - Brew

- **March** - Marsh

- **April** - Pill

- **May** - Mayonnaise

- **June** - Tune

- **July** - Lie

- **August** - Gust

- **September** - Sceptre

- **October** - Octopus

- **November** - No

- **December** - Dismember

Let's take a look at these one at a time and discuss each visualisation in turn:

JAM sounds like the start of JANuary, so you have the idea of jam, in a pot or spread over something

BREW sounds like the second part of feBRUary so there is the idea of beer, perhaps in a glass or jug

MARSH sounds like MARCH which is fairly straightforward, some kind of boggy landscape

PILL sounds like the end of aPRIL, and could refer to some kind of headache tablet

MAYONNAISE of course starts with MAY so this is easy to remember, a simple jar of mayonnaise for example

TUNE sounds almost identical to JUNE, so you have the idea of whistling harmonies

LIE is based on the end sound of the month juLY, the idea of a pair of crossed fingers to represent lying

GUST is the end sound of auGUST, the idea of a gust of wind

SCEPTRE is based on the start sound of SEPTember, a sceptre being a long ornate staff held by kings

NO is quite simply the start of the word NOvember, and is the idea of a warning, such as a 'keep out' or 'no entry' sign

DISMEMBER sounds almost exactly like DECEMBER, a rather gruesome lack of legs or arms

Reading this list just once or twice is usually enough to get most of the visualisations in your mind, but let's try to fix this information firmly in our minds with a couple of exercises.

Read the following list of months and associated images SLOWLY. Each time you read a month and it's associated image, create a visualisation of the word as vividly as you can in your mind, then move on to the next one. You may want to stare into space, or close your eyes while you imagine each of them. Take your time, there's no hurry; what is important is you give each month and associated image enough time to sink in.

Don't worry too much if you think nothing is happening or you're somehow 'doing it wrong'. Keep reading and repeating and you'll be amazed how quickly you can digest all of this.

Cold Reading Games

Here's the list. Repeat each one in your mind a few times before moving on to the next.

Remember to repeat each one in your mind before moving to the next one

January - Jam - JAMuary - a pot of jam

February - Brew - feBREWary - a beer in a glass

March - Marsh - MARSCH - a marshy bog

April - Pill - aPRIL - a headache tablet

May - Mayonnaise - MAYonnaise - a jar of mayonnaise

June - Tune - TJUNE - whistling, harmonies

July - Lie - juLIE - a fib, crossed fingers

August - Gust - auGUST - a big gust of wind

September - Scepter - SCEPTember - an ornate staff

October - Octopus - OCTOpus - an eight legged sea creature

November - No - NOvember - a warning, no entry sign

December - Dismember - DECmEMBER - chopped off legs

Now read through the list out loud before you move on. Don't forget to visualise each one - try five seconds each!

Once you've done that, let's try the next exercise without looking at the previous list to see if you can recite it from memory.

Do these ones in your head first

January goes with ...

February goes with ....

March goes with .....

April goes with ...

May goes with ....

June goes with ....

July goes with ....

August goes with ....

September goes with ....

October goes with ....

November goes with ....

December goes with ....

I think you'll be quite impressed how many of them you can remember, if not all of them.

Try the last exercise again but this time out loud, making a note of the months that slow you down.

You've got to be pretty honest with yourself here. If you are finding this pretty easy then move on, but if you are slightly unsure of some months take the time to go over them again.

Once you think you can remember most of the months and associated images without too much fuss, try this next exercise by saying out loud the months associated with each of these ideas.

Remember you need to say these ones out loud

Gust is for ......

Tune is for ....

Lie is for ....

Sceptre is for ....

Dismember is for ....

Brew is for ....

Pill is for .....

Mayonnaise is for ...

Octopus is for ....

No is for ....

Marsh is for .....

Jam is for ....

Read through the above list out loud again before you move on, filling in the month for each image.

The idea here is we're doing things in reverse by thinking of a mental image first and then calling out its associated month. The similarities in the sounds of months and images should be enough for you to recall the months fairly easily. For instance, as soon as I think of the word Marsh I know it's associated with the month March, as soon as I think of the word Jam I immediately think of January. Make sure you see each image in your mind's eye as vividly as possible.

If you find that you're still having problems then you simply need a little more practice. Try writing the months and images down on paper, or recite them while you go about your everyday business. Make your visualisations as strong as possible and don't be afraid to spend a good few seconds imprinting the months and images of each one in your mind.

Months And Signs

Let's have a quick recap of the month images before we combine everything we've learned so far

Read this list out loud again

- **January** - Jam
- **February** - Brew
- **March** - Marsh
- **April** - Pill
- **May** - Mayonnaise
- **June** - Tune
- **July** - Lie
- **August** - Gust
- **September** - Sceptre
- **October** - Octopus
- **November** - No
- **December** - Dismember

Read through the above list out loud again before you move on, and then see if you can run through it again without looking.

The month images should be sinking in by now. We're now going to combine the month images with the star signs through a series of new combined visualisations.

Here are the months and their images alongside each star sign. Have a casual read through this list, thinking about how you can connect each month's image with each star sign.

January - Jam - Capricorn - The Goat

February - Brew - Aquarius - The Water Bearer

March - Marsh - Pisces - The Fish

April - Pill - Aries - The Ram

May - Mayonnaise - Taurus - The Bull

June - Tune - Gemini - The Twins

July - Lie - Cancer - The Crab

August - Gust - Leo - The Lion

September - Sceptre - Virgo - The Virgin

October - Octopus - Libra - The Scales

November - No - Scorpio - The Scorpion

December - Dismember - Sagittarius - The Centaur

This can look a bit abstract with the months, month images and star signs all together, but with a little thought we can link these ideas up so we'll find them hard to forget.

72

Cold Reading Games

The idea is that if we can recall one, we can recall the other. For instance, if we can remember a goat (Capricorn) with a jammy beard, we can remember January. And if we can remember that May goes with mayonnaise, we can remember a bull (Taurus) eating mayonnaise.

With this in mind, imagine these next examples as vividly as you can, creating a strong mental image for each one. As with the previous visualisations you may need to close your eyes and really concentrate, but I promise you it's worth taking the time to do this properly and it still only comes down to a matter of minutes.

This bit is really important so you need to imagine each one as vividly as possible

CAPRICORN: Imagine a goat with a white beard covered in JAM standing in a grassy field

AQUARIUS: Imagine a beautiful princess pouring BEER through the air into a lake from a large vase

PISCES: Imagine two playful fish swimming in a MARSH

ARIES: Imagine an angry white ram with fiery eyes taking a PILL for his migraine

TAURUS: Imagine a strong headed bull in a fenced field licking MAYONNAISE out of a jar

GEMINI: Imagine two identical young twins holding hands in the air whistling a TUNE together

CANCER: Imagine a big red crab on a sandy beach telling a LIE (crossing its claws as if it's fibbing)

LEO: Imagine a great lion with a fiery mane blown by a GUST of wind as it surveys its territory

VIRGO: Imagine an innocent young girl in a flowery field holding a SCEPTRE

LIBRA: Imagine an empty pair of scales weighing nothing but air held by an OCTOPUS

SCORPIO: Imagine a scorpion scuttling about on the sand near an oasis with a NO entry sign

SAGITTARIUS: Imagine a centaur with no legs (DISMEMBER) firing a flaming arrow from a bow

Once you've got to the end of this list, go back and re-visualise each of them one more time.

And then, once you've gone through this process twice, try and forget everything. You'll understand why later.

(Feel free to have a third go around if you like, but don't forget that once you're finished I want you to try and forget everything you've just imagined!)

Of course, forgetting everything you've just imagined is almost impossible, simply because it's very hard to forget things you've put the time into imagining. The main problem with people who say they have a bad memory is not that they can't recall things that they've learned, it's that they've not put enough creative effort into learning things in the first place.

Top Tip: If your head is hurting from doing all that visualisation, take a break. You'll be amazed how much you can remember hours or days from now, even though you've only done these exercises a few times.

Now let's see if this has been of any use. Here are some questions, see how well you do.

See the object in your mind and let the greater picture come to you - it shouldn't take too much effort

Which star sign has a beard covered in jam?
Which star sign is pouring beer into a lake?
Which star sign is swimming in a marsh?
Which star sign is taking a headache pill?
Which star sign is licking a jar of mayonnaise?
Which star sign is whistling a tune in harmony?
Which star sign is telling a lie?
Which star sign is having its hair blown by a gust of wind?
Which star sign is holding a sceptre?
Which star sign is an octopus holding?
Which star sign is holding a no entry sign?
Which star sign has its legs missing?

You may find that you can recall the visual image in your mind for many of these, but you can't recall the name of the star sign itself. Not to worry. Mark down the star signs whose names you find more difficult than others and have a go at re-visualising them before having another go at the list.

What should become apparent is that some of the signs are extremely well matched with the words given for each month:

February has the word BREW so it's easy to remember that it's Aquarius The Water Bearer pouring beer instead of water

March has the word MARSH so it's obvious that Pisces The Fish should be swimming in it

November simply has the word NO, if there's one sign you shouldn't go near it's Scorpio The Scorpion!

Now go back to the start of this section and read it all over again if you haven't already, repeating the exercises before moving on.

We're now going to try the previous questions but in a different order

Don't stress out too much about answering these questions, just relax and let the answers come to you

Which star sign has its legs missing?
Which star sign is pouring beer into a lake?
Which star sign is holding a sceptre?
Which star sign is an octopus holding?
Which star sign is swimming in a marsh?
Which star sign has a white beard covered in jam?
Which star sign is taking a headache pill?
Which star sign is licking a jar of mayonnaise?
Which star sign is having its hair blown by a gust of wind?
Which star sign is holding a no entry sign?
Which star sign is whistling a harmonious tune?
Which star sign is telling a lie?

By this point you should be getting the hang of this. When you visualise one of the month words its associated star sign should be arriving in your mind pretty much simultaneously. You now have a combined mental image for each sign; they're one and the same.

The 23rd Day Premise

Each star sign starts around the 23rd day of the month and ends on the 22nd of the next month. This is a generalisation as the start and end times shift between the 19th and 23rd depending on the month involved. The dates between the changeover from one star sign to another are called the 'cusp'. For our purposes and to achieve almost 90% accuracy with as little memory work as possible, we're going to pretend that all signs start on the 23rd and run through to the 22nd of the next month, something I call 'The 23rd Day Premise'.

Using this idea, our inaccurate list of star signs will fall on these dates:

• 23rd December to 22nd January - Capricorn
• 23rd January to 22nd February - Aquarius
• 23rd February to 22nd March - Pisces
• 23rd March to 22nd April - Aries
• 23rd April to 22nd May - Taurus
• 23rd May to 22nd June - Gemini
• 23rd June to 22nd July - Cancer
• 23rd July to 22nd August - Leo
• 23rd August to 22nd September - Virgo
• 23rd September to 22nd October - Libra
• 23rd October to 22nd November - Scorpio
• 23rd November to 22rd December - Sagittarius

As you can see, Capricorn mostly belongs to January, but starts at the end of December. Aquarius mostly belongs to February, but starts at the end of January, etc. All star signs end in the months they inhabit the most.

With so many dates this can still appear a little confusing, so let's just concentrate on the months each sign has the most days in:

• January - Capricorn
• February - Aquarius
• March - Pisces
• April - Aries
• May - Taurus
• June - Gemini
• July - Cancer
• August - Leo
• September - Virgo
• October - Libra
• November - Scorpio
• December - Sagittarius

This is all you need to know, simply pretending that each sign starts on the 23rd of the month. Capricorn 'belongs' to January, Aquarius 'belongs' to February etc. These are the visualisations and connections you have already memorised in the previous sections of course.

Close But No Cigar

So how can we use the 23rd Day Premise? Well, if all star signs started on the 23rd of their respective months, we'd know this much:

1. If someone's birthday falls before the 23rd of any given month, their star sign is from the same month

2. If someone's birthday falls on or after the 23rd of any given month, their star sign is from the next month

For Example

- If someone told you they were born on October 2nd, you'd know straight away that their star sign was from the same month

- If someone told you they were born on December 28th, you'd know straight away that their star sign is from the next month, January

- If someone told you they were born on April 18th, you'd know straight away that their star sign was from the same month

- If someone told you they were born on July 24th, you'd know straight away that their star sign is from the next month, August

- If someone told you they were born on January 5th, you'd know straight away that their star sign was from the same month

So the rule for remembering which month to use for someone's star sign is:

Use the current month's star sign before the 23rd, otherwise use the next month's sign.

By knowing this, and with what we're already learned to visualise, we can now instantly calculate anyone's star sign from their birth date. Well, nearly, because by pretending that each start sign starts on the 23rd of each month we can only be 87% accurate, simply because the signs vary their start dates between the 19th and the 23rd of each month as we have discussed.

How to put The 23rd Day Premise into practice:

1. Find out someone's date of birth
2. If the DAY they were born is before the 23rd of the month, they take the star sign from the same month; otherwise the next
3. Think of the month word for the relevant month and you'll immediately know what star sign they are

That's it!

Example One

Someone tells you they were born on the 10th of July. They were born on the 10th which is before the 23rd so you keep the month. The month image for July is LIE and you immediately see Cancer The Crab lying with its claws crossed. The person is a Cancer.

Example Two

Someone tells you they were born on the 25th of January. The 25th is after the 23rd so you use the next month, February. You think of the month image for February which is BREW. The moment you think of brew you can see Aquarius The Water Bearer pouring beer into a lake. The person is an Aquarius.

That sounds quite lengthy, but it can go very fast indeed with a small amount of practice. The moment you have the correct month image you jump straight to the associated visualisation and see the relevant star sign. The important thing you have to remember is to go forwards a month if the day the person was born on falls on or after the 23rd. As about three quarters of all star signs start before the 23rd you'll only be going forward to the next month roughly a quarter of the time.

Let's test how good you are at this. Answer these questions as if every star sign started on the 23rd of the month. What is each person's star sign? Don't forget, go forward a month if the day is on or after the 23rd of the month, otherwise use the month you're on. And then remember the word that goes with the month you are left with.

EXERCISE ONE - RECALL - One minute total, five seconds each

Take your time, it will get easier with practice!

I was born on the 24th of January. What star sign am I?
I was born on the 5th February. What star sign am I?
I was born on the 30th March. What star sign am I?
I was born on the 15th April. What star sign am I?
I was born on the 2nd May. What star sign am I?
I was born on the 9th June. What star sign am I?
I was born on the 24th July. What star sign am I?
I was born on the 1st August. What star sign am I?
I was born on the 25th September. What star sign am I?
I was born on the 20th October. What star sign am I?
I was born on the 30th November. What star sign am I?
I was born on the 4th December. What star sign am I?

After attempting those twelve questions you should be getting a feel for how the star signs overlap the end of one month and the majority of the next. You should also be getting the hang of working out fairly rapidly whether you need to go forward a month or not.

Let's do things in reverse just once to make sure we're joining everything up properly in our minds. To do the next exercise you're going to have to think of the mental image you have of a star sign, see the month word in that image, and then convert it back into its actual month.

EXERCISE TWO - RECALL - Two minutes total, ten seconds each

This is a bit easier than the last exercise, but still good practice!

I'm a Capricorn. What month does my star sign start in?
I'm a Sagittarius. What month does my star sign start in?
I'm a Scorpio. What month does my star sign start in?
I'm an Aries. What month does my star sign start in?
I'm a Pisces. What month does my star sign start in?
I'm an Aquarius. What month does my star sign start in?
I'm a Cancer. What month does my star sign start in?
I'm a Gemini. What month does my star sign start in?
I'm a Taurus. What month does my star sign start in?
I'm a Libra. What month does my star sign start in?
I'm a Virgo. What month does my star sign start in?
I'm a Leo. What month does my star sign start in?

That's it! If you can get through these questions without too much difficulty then you'll find it hard to ever forget the links you've created between the months and the images associated with each sign. With just a quick bit of revision every now and again you should be able to remember the months for each star sign at the drop of a hat.

Bonus Chapter II - The Classic Reading

The classic reading is a series of twelve lines that apply to almost everybody due to their vague and open nature, known also as 'Forer Statements' after the psychologist Bertram R. Forer who compiled them from tabloid horoscopes in the late 1940s. He proved that people have a tendency to 'read into' these generalisations, imbuing them with their own relevance simply because they'd been led to believe the statements were of a personal nature.

Knowing these lines won't suddenly turn you into a great reader, but it's useful to know of their existence as they can offer enough mental stimulus to get you out of a situation when you've run out of things to say for one reason or another. Have a read through the twelve lines as if they were written specifically for you as a personality test, and see which ones you agree with.

1. You have a great need for other people to like and admire you.

2. You have a tendency to be critical of yourself.

3. You have a great deal of unused capacity which you have not turned to your advantage.

4. While you have some personality weaknesses, you are generally able to compensate for them.

5. Your sexual adjustment has presented problems for you.

6. Disciplined and self-controlled outside, you tend to be worrisome and insecure inside.

7. At times you have serious doubts as to whether you have made the right decision or done the right thing.

8. You prefer a certain amount of change and variety and become dissatisfied when hemmed in by restrictions and limitations.

9. You pride yourself as an independent thinker and do not accept others' statements without satisfactory proof.

10. You have found it unwise to be too frank in revealing yourself to others.

11. At times you are extroverted, affable, sociable, while at other times you are introverted, wary, reserved.

12. Some of your aspirations tend to be pretty unrealistic.

You'll find that these lines are as true now as they've ever been, empty hooks we can easily hang attributes onto. They'll never go out of date, they simply aren't specific enough! Most people like a bit of admiration, we're all critical of ourselves to some degree and I'm sure you, as well as I, have some unused capacity hiding within which you have not turned to your advantage...

If you can get a few of these lines in to your head you'll find their structure can come in handy when you're giving a reading and want to add a bit of spice. Most of these lines could easily be attributed to a line on the hand during a conversation, or a squiggle in someone's handwriting. One of the interesting things is that as you get better at giving readings you'll find yourself talking like this quite often.

As readings in the context of this book are less about specifics and more about helping people understand their own personality you'll find yourself continuously making vague statements, which only find some shape with the help of the person you are reading for. It's not that people are gullible, far from it; we are meaning makers, we internalise everything, and we all would really like to understand ourselves more. Helping someone to do that is not a bad thing. See line number 7 above? That explains a lot! Study the twelve lines and take some time to think about the way you approach the language of giving a reading.

In my book 'The James Bond Cold Reading' I outline a way of remembering and using these lines for maximum impact, so if you want to know more about this branch of cold reading you could do worse than give it a look.

Bonus Chapter III - Cartomancy

Some of the concepts in this chapter are taken from my book Cartomancy - Fortune Telling With Playing Cards.

If you've got this far then there a good chance you've become fairly familiar with the numerology chapter and have a pretty good grasp of the meanings of the numbers 1 thru 10. If that's the case then you're in a fortunate position because many other readings systems are derived from numerology, none more so than playing card readings, otherwise known as cartomancy.

Although there's less chance of a pack of cards turning up while you're out socialising (heaven forbid you actually take one out with you) you shouldn't rule it out. Instead of doing a useless card trick why not be different and read someone's cards? If you already know the meanings of the numbers 1 to 10 you're more than halfway there; with only four suits that run from 1 to 10 each you'll already know the meanings of 40 cards!

Suit Meanings

The suit meanings are pretty self explanatory, no more so than hearts and diamonds.

DIAMONDS - Money
HEARTS - Love
CLUBS - Work
SPADES - Obstacles

Clubs and spades are slightly more abstract than the red cards, but if you imagine going to work to smash rocks as a caveman with a CLUB in your hand, and imagine that someone has dug a hole and has left a SPADE beside it which is getting in your way you'll find the black cards pretty easy to remember too.

Card Meanings

As we already know the meanings of the numbers one to ten, we need only superimpose their meanings onto each suit to give each card their own unique attribute. I won't list each and every card here as that would be missing the point; the idea is to come up with meanings for each card as you go by fusing the idea of the number with the idea of the suit.

Look through these examples and take a moment to see how I've come up with a description for each, using the meanings of the numbers and suits in tandem.

Examples

Three Of Diamonds

With the expansion and new creation of the three, and the power and success of diamonds, this card really stands out as a card showing new ventures taking shape.

Nine Of Diamonds

With the dynamic nine signifying things moving rapidly and successfully in the right direction with a current project, and the financial success of diamonds, this card is extremely fortuitous and shows the rapid and rewarding developments of existing undertakings.

Ten Of Diamonds

Signifying the successful completion of a project or existing life cycle, with the rewards and power of diamonds, this is a tremendously auspicious card. Like all tens, it is about completion and therefore the end of one cycle and start of another.

Five Of Clubs

With the organic growth of the five with the work aspect of clubs, this card brings to mind the idea of things really taking shape at work - from solid foundations things are really starting to grow and develop.

Nine Of Clubs

With the nine signifying things coming to fruition, and the social and work aspects of clubs, this card is a strong indicator of work plans coming together and social engagements taking a front seat.

Ten Of Clubs

With the end of a cycle and the goals being reached, with the work ethic of clubs, it's no surprise that this is possibly one of the best work related cards in the deck, the completion of long term projects and successful ventures.

Two Of Hearts

We know that the two is about partnerships and sharing, and with the Hearts influence, also about love and pleasure, it is no surprise to find that the two of hearts is one of the most romantic cards in the pack and is a strong indicator of good relationships and happy marriages.

Three Of Hearts

With the idea of partnerships bearing fruit, and the love and romance aspect of hearts, this card can't help but be a romantic card but with the added possibility of love turning into much more - a child on the horizon perhaps? Or if not romance, the development of partnerships into fruitful relationships that go much deeper.

Seven Of Hearts

With the mystical and higher thinking seven, and the love aspect of hearts, this is a very spiritual card and can mean a breakthrough in all things spiritual, or of pure matters of the heart and soul - the kind of happiness that can only come from within - or above!

Nine Of Spades

With nine signifying great movement near the end of a project and the spades signifying obstacles, this card shows that the last few steps of a current endeavour may well be extremely challenging and one should look out for last minute snags and surprises.

Ten Of Spades

With the ten being all about the successful completion of goals, yet spades signifying hurdles and fights, this card is possibly the most conflicted in the deck. As it stands, it is quite hard to read this card alone and care must be taken to see this card in context with the rest of the reading. One positive aspect of this card is that the ten is the end of a cycle and that after times of great upheaval comes the chance to start anew.

The Four Aces

The Aces are all about the energy of starting - of raw drive and will. Consequently they 'energise' the suits that they are coupled with. The Ace of Diamonds is about the pure force of money and power, the Ace of Clubs is all about the strength and determination of work and growth, the Ace of Hearts is the essence of love and emotions, and the Ace of Spades is the power of the warrior to take on anything. These cards are somewhat naive - they are the raw power of each suit before steps have been taken - and as such they effect all the cards around them with their idealistic and unquestioned power.

If you want to practice making up your own meanings, simply pick up a pack of playing cards and deal them out one at a time, saying something about each one as you go. You'll be amazed what you come up with.

Face Cards

As many people know and believe, the face cards in a deck refer to people. The jacks represent younger people of no particular sex and may also indicate news, whereas the queens and kings are female and male respectively.

HEART face cards represent friends, lovers and family
DIAMOND face cards represent people with money or influence
CLUB face cards represent people in the work place
SPADES represent people who get in your way

Of course, these meanings for the face cards simply reflect the meanings of each suit. For instance, spades represent obstacles so it stands to reason that a spade face card will be someone who is blocking your way.

Giving A Reading

I'm not going to go into the ins and outs of giving a full blown card reading reading here; if you've followed through this book and learned to find 'gold', you'll have no problems finding it when you're giving a playing card reading.

A simple way to structure a reading is to get someone to shuffle a deck and pick out just three cards. If you lay them in a row from left to right you have their past, present and future cards. By looking at these cards and examining the way they interact with each other you can come up with a pretty interesting reading using what you've learned in this short chapter.

With a three card reading it's useful to use the idea that each card influences the previous card. So card two influences card one, and card three influences card two.

Example One

Three Of Clubs / Six Of Diamonds / Four Of Spades

The reading starts with the Three of Clubs, which is all about ideas taking shape in and around work - the 'expansion' of the number Three with the influence of the Club - the work and socialising suit. With the Three of Clubs as the focus and the Six of Diamonds as the influence we have the positive and strong ideas of communication and money. It could be that things are looking up regarding these work ideas taking shape and if there hasn't been news about an injection of money as yet it could come soon. As the Six is about communication and the Diamonds are about money and power this is all quite a good influence on the Three of Clubs.

Moving on to the Six of Diamonds we can see that this is influenced by the Four of Spades. The four is home life related, and as a Spade this spells trouble at home influencing the communication and money aspect of the Six of Diamonds. Perhaps there's some problem with work creating friction at home, or it could be that the sources of the money are themselves being restricted by home life and other commitments. Whatever it is, it's obviously something that has to be sorted out before things can move on..

Example Two

Five Of Spades / Four Of Hearts / Jack Of Diamonds

The reading starts with the Five of Spades, the five signifying growth at home and in things that are already formed, but as it's a Spade this is a problem with development and could mean there's some kind of stagnation going on. With the focus on the Five of Spades and the influence of the Four of Hearts, we have the stability of the four with love and warmth of the Heart coming to bear on this problem. This is not a bad thing - it looks like whatever is getting stuck somewhere is going to be helped with loved ones at home.

With the focus on the Four of Hearts and with the influence of the Jack of Diamonds we know that there is a young person involved who is responsible for this stability and help. This could be an outside influence or could be a member of the family. If it's an outside influence then their help could be monetary, and if it's family then their powerful influence could be of the helping and healing kind.

The Jack could also be news, possibly involving a young person, that is part of this helping and stabilising Four of Hearts. It could be that news will come from someone that is expected but has yet to be known, and it is this that alleviates the symptoms of the Five of Spades.

Cold Reading Games

Other books by Julian Moore

Palmistry - Palm Readings In Your Own Words

Graphology - The Art Of Handwriting Analysis

Numerology - Numbers Past And Present With The Lo Shu Square

Star Signs - A Cool System For Remembering The Dates And Meanings Of The Twelve Signs Of The Zodiac

The James Bond Cold Reading

Cartomancy - Fortune Telling With Playing Cards

TO DOWNLOAD THE

CHEAT SHEET

SIMPLY REGISTER THIS BOOK HERE:

http://www.thecoldreadingcompany.co.uk/coldreading/crgreg

You'll need to use your computer and not your ebook reader!

On registration you will receive an email with a link to the **PDF** download.

Either print it out onto index cards, or upload it into your mobile phone so you can take a quick refresher with you everywhere you go!

(So there's no excuse to forget this stuff!)

Made in the USA
San Bernardino, CA
29 April 2016